Second Read

Columbia Journalism Review Books

SERIES EDITORS: **VICTOR NAVASKY, EVAN CORNOG,** AND THE EDITORS OF THE *COLUMBIA JOURNALISM REVIEW*

Second Read

Writers Look Back at Classic Works of Reportage

EDITED BY **JAMES MARCUS** *AND THE* **STAFF** *OF THE*
COLUMBIA JOURNALISM REVIEW

COLUMBIA UNIVERSITY PRESS *New York*

COLUMBIA UNIVERSITY PRESS
PUBLISHERS SINCE 1893

New York   Chichester, West Sussex
cup.columbia.edu

Library of Congress Cataloging-in-Publication Data

Second read : writers look back at classic works of reportage / edited by James Marcus
and the staff of the Columbia Journalism Review.

p. cm. — (Columbia journalism review books)

ISBN 978-0-231-15930-2 (cloth : alk. paper) — ISBN 978-0-231-15931-9 (pbk.) — ISBN
978-0-231-50058-6 (electronic)

1. American prose literature—20th century—History and criticism. 2. Reportage
literature, American—History and criticism. 3. Journalism—United States—History—20th
century. I. Marcus, James, 1959– II. Columbia Journalism Review. III. Title.

PS366.R44S43   2012

818'.508039—dc23   2011020757

Columbia University Press books are printed on permanent and durable acid-free paper.

This book was printed on paper with recycled content.

Printed in the United States of America

C 10 9 8 7 6 5 4 3 2 1

P 10 9 8 7 6 5 4 3 2 1

Interior design by **MARTIN N. HINZE**

Contents

Introduction

JAMES MARCUS

"Curiously enough," Vladimir Nabokov once observed, "one cannot read a book: one can only reread it." Nabokov, whose appetite for the delicious detail in any work of prose made him a ceaseless advocate of rereading, was mainly talking about fiction. But his comment applies equally to nonfiction.

The first time we read a great piece of reportage, we may be swept away by its narrative dash or fact-finding ardor. Only when we go back to it, days or years or decades later, do we discover its hidden charms. The second time through, we latch onto the reflexive, glinting irony in Peter Fleming's *Brazilian Adventure* or the surrealistic touches in Gabriel García Márquez's *The Story of a Shipwrecked Sailor*. John McPhee's *Annals of the Former World* suddenly seems a warmer work, less about auriferous gravels and more about the people who study them. And only in retrospect do we recognize Cornelius Ryan's *The Longest Day* as a precursor of the New Journalistic fireworks that were to follow.

With these thoughts in mind, the *Columbia Journalism Review* launched its Second Read series in 2004. The idea was to get distinguished journalists to look back at the books that truly fired their imagination—the books, often, that made them want to be journalists in the first place. We had no particular syllabus to construct: the authors chose their subjects on the basis of pure enthusiasm. Yet the essays gathered in this collection do amount to a snapshot history of mid-century American journalism (with a handful of chronological and geographical outliers). The major events and upheavals are all here, captured by many of the century's most memorable voices: the Great Depression, World War II, the assassination of JFK, the ideological earthquake of the late sixties, the rise of environmentalism, and the perpetual skirmishing of identity politics.

Second Read also suggests a number of contrasting models for contemporary journalism. Should reporters be participants in the events they are covering, or even (if we are to follow the trails blazed by Tom Wolfe and Norman Mailer) characters in their own stories? Or should they stick to a more traditional conception of reportorial conduct, in which the journalist assembles a hoard of factual material without ever showing his or her hand? When Rachel Carson wrote *Silent Spring*, she was very much an advocate, and the same thing could be said of Palagummi Sainath, who set out to prick India's communal conscience with *Everybody Loves a Good Drought*. But when A. J. Liebling zeroed in on Earl Long's electoral shenanigans, he seemed intent on suspending judgment—on presenting the florid facts and nothing more. As journalism enters a new century (and incidentally, as *CJR* celebrates its fiftieth year of publication, in 2011), there is no single, satisfactory path to follow. Instead there are many, and we hope this collection will function as something of a road map.

* * *

The Second Read series got under way with Rick Perlstein's essay on Paul Cowan's *The Tribes of America*, which had been published in 1979 and out of print for decades. Here, argued Perlstein, was a penetrating study of America's culture wars, written many years before that phrase was even coined. He gave Cowan plenty of credit for his prescience. He gave him even more credit for questioning his own cultural assumptions as a lefty correspondent for the *Village Voice*:

> What Paul Cowan understood long before anyone else was that there was a new kind of story to tell about such conflicts: that attempts to "coax people into the melting pot" had costs as well as benefits, and [such] campaigns . . . must not simply be imposed

by fiat. Cowan understood how "often people I might once have written off as reactionaries were fighting to preserve their cultural and their psychological and their physical turf," and that this new argument over the meaning of democracy was defining the next frontier of political conflict itself. That America had tribes, and that sometimes—often—they would come to blows.

In this case, Perlstein not only drew attention to a neglected classic. He also inspired the New Press to usher *The Tribes of America* back into print in 2007, with his essay as an introduction.

Several other pieces in the collection perform a similar feat of rediscovery, shining a light on works that have fallen victim to shifts in literary taste or ideological fashion. There is, for example, John Maxwell Hamilton's essay on Vincent Sheean's *Personal History*. Sheean, a swashbuckling foreign correspondent of the old school, was a looming figure during the thirties. His memoir won the very first National Book Award for nonfiction in 1935 and ascended to the upper reaches of the pop-culture pantheon when Alfred Hitchcock adapted it (very loosely) for *Foreign Correspondent* in 1940. Yet Sheean's intensity, and his willingness not only to report but also to interpret the world for his readers, eventually fell out of style. Hamilton makes a powerful argument for his resurrection.

Claire Dederer is equally ardent about another lost classic of reportage, Betty MacDonald's *Anybody Can Do Anything*. In this case, the author is not a complete obscurity: her earlier memoir *The Egg and I*, as well as her children's books, won her a fair measure of fame during the forties. But her chronicle of Seattle during the Great Depression, when she kept her family afloat with a succession of increasingly hardscrabble jobs, has long since fallen off the radar. Dederer praises it as "a rough draft of history. The details of home and work life accrue, anecdotes pile up, and suddenly the reader has a real sense of daily existence in the West during the 1930s. This is a cheerful, unassuming way of documenting a socially and economically turbulent period. But it's documentation nonetheless."

Readers will encounter similar advocacy from Robert Lipsyte (stumping for Paul Gallico's *Farewell to Sport*) and Justin Peters (whose pitch on behalf of Peter Fleming's *Brazilian Adventure* puts this comic gem in its proper context: the stuffy, self-inflating narratives penned by dilettante explorers of the last century). Here, argue the authors, are books that never should have fallen into limbo in the first place. Perhaps one or more of them will now follow *The Tribes of America* back into print.

Elsewhere, the authors address books whose classic status has made them almost *too* familiar. Dale Maharidge argues that James Agee's high style and sociological fervor in *Let Us Now Praise Famous Men* have obscured the real core of that book's magic: the author's emotional connection with his subjects. "Agee embodies passion and soul," we read, "two qualities that some editors fear because they mistakenly equate them with bias, or having an agenda when covering the human side of social issues. Agee was not about doing journalism. He was about living it."

In a related vein, Connie Schultz now sees Michael Herr's celebrated *Dispatches* as not only a nightmarish account of the Vietnam War, but also an index of that conflict's very inscrutability, its refusal to be boiled down to wonkish policy points: "Thirty years after reading the book for the first time, I still have the same gut response: at least I understand why I will never understand what happened to our boys in Vietnam." And Marla Cone argues for the perennial value of Rachel Carson's *Silent Spring*, long after the specific targets of her crusading environmental polemic (DDT, PCBs) have been banned.

There are also several thematic threads running through the entire collection. One is the allure (and potential pitfalls) of participatory journalism. When Ted Conover first encountered Stanley Booth's *The True Adventures of the Rolling Stones* in 1984, he was researching a book of his own on Mexican immigrants. Booth's absolute commitment to immersion journalism—which entailed smoking, snorting, and injecting the very same drugs as his subjects, a process that may have delayed delivery of the manuscript by many years—made a huge impression on Conover. So did the digressive tone.

"Maybe because those early days were also a time when I often found myself stuck in writing," he recalls, "too self-critical and unable to find the words, Booth's book also came to hold a sort of magic for me, the power to break a dam and start a flow. Which is more, somehow, than I can say for most books I admire."

Participatory journalism was also the lure of Gallico's *Farewell to Sport*, at least the first time Robert Lipsyte encountered the book in 1953. Gallico "swam with Johnny Weismuller, golfed with Bobby Jones, and lasted less than two minutes in the ring with Jack Dempsey." And even when he wasn't engaging in these pre-Plimptonian antics, Gallico wrote about sports as a consummate insider. He inspired the young Lipsyte to follow the same career track. Yet when Lipsyte read the book a second time in 1975, he was dismayed by the author's casual racism and flabby ethics. ("What an old whore he was, always begging Babe Ruth or Gene Tunney to show up at some event he was promoting. How did that affect his coverage?") Only his third encounter with the book, which inspired his 2006 *CJR* essay, finally put it all in perspective. Given the brave new world of steroids, NASCAR, and Tiger Woods, Lipstye is confident that Gallico would have found "a way to walk the line with style, confidence, and residuals."

There is also a fascination with the impact of New Journalism—and an ongoing effort to identify its precursors. Michael Shapiro sees the earliest glimmers of New Journalistic density and detail in an unlikely source: Cornelius Ryan's *The Longest Day*. What he finds most inspiring is Ryan's devotion to *reporting*, which none other than Tom Wolfe identified as the wellspring of the journalist's craft. Shapiro describes how Ryan's infatuation with sheer facticity shaped his own career at a crucial juncture:

> I began to understand that while my writing would after a time improve only incrementally, reporting was a craft that could, if done ambitiously, remain beyond perfecting. The lonely and maddening business of writing could be fueled not by what dexterity with words I could summon but by all the many things I had to find out. I fell in love with reporting only after I was old enough to appreciate that, journalistically speaking, it could keep me young.

Thomas Mallon follows the same trail back to another book, William Manchester's *The Death of a President*. Again, he's not claiming that Manchester anticipated the zingy, hyperventilating prose identified with the New Journalists, nor their habit of parachuting into their pieces as virtual characters. It's the factual impasto that Manchester builds up, and his dramatic (one might even say cinematic) reconstruction of very contemporary scenes, that does the trick for Mallon:

> Manchester was working in the period when writers like Tom Wolfe and Jimmy Breslin—Capote too, for that matter—were giving New Journalism its gaudy birth. *The Death of a President*

is, of course, a work of history, by an author reconstructing rather than participating in events. Still, the history is so recent and the techniques so similar to Wolfe and Co.'s that one wonders why Breslin's piece about the digging of Kennedy's grave has become a textbook example of the genre while Manchester goes unmentioned in Marc Weingarten's study of New Journalism, *The Gang That Wouldn't Write Straight*.

Who got there first is ultimately a parlor game, of course. What matters is how the lessons of New Journalism (now approaching the grizzled age of fifty, and not so new anymore) have been absorbed and modified by subsequent generations of journalists. In fact, that matters quite a lot. At the moment, there is a real tension between narrative flair, always a calling card of the New Journalists, and old-fashioned accuracy in reporting.

What's more, we are in an age deeply suspicious of journalistic objectivity, not to mention journalistic accuracy. Along these lines, Nicholson Baker finds some fascinating lessons in Daniel Defoe's *A Journal of the Plague Year*, published in 1722:

> The hoaxers and the embellishers, the fake autobiographers, look on Defoe as a kind of patron saint. Defoe lied a lot. But he also hated his lying habit, at least sometimes. He said the lying made a hole in the heart. About certain events he wanted truth told. And one event he really cared about was the great plague of 1665, which happened when he was about five years old.

Baker himself argues for a strict demarcation between fact and fiction. Not for him the fuzzy boundary so often evoked by our contemporary apostles of truthiness: political fakers, fraudulent memoirists, pilfering academics. Yet Defoe's production leaves him strangely conflicted. The book is something of a sham, with a bogus first-person narrator who never existed. Yet this ersatz memoir *moves* Baker: "The book feels like something heartfelt, that grew out of decades of accumulated notes and memories—although written with impressive speed. It doesn't feel like an artificial swizzle of falsifications."

Meanwhile, Connie Schultz, no less moved by *Dispatches*, wrestles with the subsequent discovery that Herr's book too is marbled with inventions and secondhand reportage. An instinctive stickler for the truth, she also decides to cut the author some slack: "I have never had the guts to cover a war, and doubt I could ever risk my safety, and my sanity, as Herr did when he was in Vietnam. I have neither the right nor the will to pass judgment on how he brought home the war to millions of Americans who had yet to face it."

Neither of these pieces, it should be repeated, is an endorsement for slippery reporting. What they do acknowledge is that we are sometimes willing (or at least tempted) to let journalists cut expedient corners in the name of vividness, urgency, intensity. We want the sort of thrilling cultural diagnostics David Ulin sees in Didion's *Slouching Towards Bethlehem*, which explore "the yawning gap between who we are and who we think we are, between those stories we tell ourselves and the ways we actually live." We want to *be there*, and may be willing to sacrifice something for this full-body immersion. Whether this represents a step forward or backward is a question that readers of this collection will be eager to debate—one, we hope, of many.

Second Read

Rick Perlstein

PAUL COWAN'S
THE TRIBES OF AMERICA

In the fall of 1974, in Kanawha County, West Virginia, Christian fundamentalists enraged at the imposition of "blasphemous" textbooks in the public schools demolished a wing of a school board building with fifteen sticks of dynamite. When the board insisted on keeping the books in the curriculum, homes were bombed and school buses shot at. "Jesus Wouldn't Have Read Them," read one of the slogans of a movement whose leader, a preacher, would soon face charges of conspiracy to bomb two elementary schools.

Into this whirlwind stepped Paul Cowan, a shaggy-haired, bespectacled, left-wing New York Jew, trying to make sense of why he felt sympathy for the side that was laying the dynamite.

For people like Cowan, a thirty-four-year-old staff writer at *The Village Voice*, it was a boom time for existential drift. In 1970 he published *The Making of an Un-American*, the memoir of a raw and arrogant new-left punk who had taken a one-year leave from the *Voice* in 1966 for a stint in the Peace Corps that was supposed to be broadening, but ended up being wildly disillusioning. "When I read that the Viet Cong had attacked the American embassy in Saigon during the Tet offensive," Cowan concluded in *Un-American*, "I was almost able to imagine that I was a member of the raiding party." But by the time Cowan began his next project, in 1971, life inside the new left had become an emotional burden for him: diminishing returns, dashed certitudes, "intellectual claustrophobia." That was how, "gradually, half-consciously, without any theory or any plan, I decided to cross the sound barrier of dogma and test my beliefs against the realities of American life." The twelve chapters of *The Tribes of America* (1979) were the felicitous result.

A person of Cowan's inclinations and background was supposed to know exactly what to think about a howling mob gathered around a crucifix-emblazoned flag and expectorating demands to burn books of the sort the reporter would want his kids to study, books with chapters by Norman Mailer and James Baldwin and test questions asking students to interpret rather than parrot what they had read. It would have been easy to record the scenes of bonfires and leave it at that; certainly that would have satisfied Cowan's readers back in Greenwich Village. Instead, Cowan took the riskier step: wondering whether these criminals didn't also have a point.

The people responsible for the textbooks were bureaucrats who wrote blithely of pedagogy's power to "induce changes . . . in the behavior of the 'culturally lost' of Appalachia," and identified teachers as state-designated "change agents" and schools as "the experimental center, and the core of this design." Nowadays the arrogance of this formulation is as grating to us as a chalkboard screech. Not then. It was an era when the language of universally applicable liberal enlightenment flew trippingly off cosmopolitan tongues. Which was why it came as such a shock when the "culturally lost" proved to have ideas of their own—that their culture had inherent dignity and value, and that textbooks suggesting that Christian revelation was on a par with Greek myth were, as protesters put it, "moral genocide."

It took a keen eye and an open mind to recognize that the cosmopolitans were pursuing a form of class warfare. Cowan noticed how urban and suburban professionals in Kanawha County—"Hillers," in local parlance—spoke nervously in private of how familiarity with names like Mailer and Baldwin would get their precious darlings into Harvard and keep them out of West Virginia Tech. The Hillers weren't about to risk having their upward climb impeded by the "Creekers," poor residents in the hollows who wanted "to protest corruption," as one suburbanite told Cowan, but didn't "even know how to spell that word." But some Creekers were motivated by similar dreams of upward mobility. Their version of it was just incompatible with the Hillers' impositions—like the kid who told

Cowan "he wanted to go to West Virginia Tech, to be an engineer," and he felt he needed "a good basic education" to do it.

Dynamite wasn't the answer. But neither was a kind of cultural imperialism indifferent to the fact that 81 percent of the district opposed the textbooks. It was, in a word, complicated. Certainly more complicated than the portraits other journalists were creating for sneering consumption back home: death threats, double-barreled shotguns, "Onward, Christian Soldiers." The futile last stand of yokels against the inevitable march of progress.

It was a time when, certainly to the left, local cultures were of keenest interest as obstacles federal judges eradicated in order to deliver social justice. But what Paul Cowan understood long before anyone else was that there was a new kind of story to tell about such conflicts: that attempts to "coax people into the melting pot" had costs as well as benefits, and campaigns to replace "our periods with your question marks," as one Creeker put it with aphoristic intelligence, must not simply be imposed by fiat. Cowan understood how "often, people I might once have written off as reactionaries were fighting to preserve their culture and their psychological and physical turf," and that this new argument over the meaning of democracy was defining the next frontier of political conflict itself. That America had tribes, and that sometimes—often—they would come to blows.

We call those fights the "culture wars" now, and we have a more richly variegated vocabulary to describe the Hillers and the Creekers: blue state and red state. Yuppie and redneck. New Class and white working class. Liberal and evangelical. We describe our nation's dueling dreads over such concepts with a casualness that once marked cocktail party chatter about the inevitability of consensus liberalism. Writing in the 1970s, however, Cowan had no such clichés to lean on. He had to figure it out for himself. He did so brilliantly—eyes open, with a courage I can scarcely believe. He traveled all over the country: to Boston during the busing wars; to Forest Hills, Queens, where he was shocked at the racism of immigrant Jews fighting the construction of a low-income housing project; to the southernmost border of the United States, where the sacrifices Mexicans were making to preserve their families looked like anarchy to the Americans patrolling the border with shotguns. Cowan's reporting from these places left him "with a profound respect for the stability of religion, of ceremony, of family life: of customs I'd once regarded as old-fashioned and bourgeois." His travels also found him realizing that "those same longings, translated into political terms, have produced the vicious fights I've witnessed for the past seven years and recorded in this book." His agonized sensitivity to battlefields then barely emergent makes for one of the most remarkable books I have ever read by any journalist.

It was courage that allowed him to achieve it, though courage of a certain sort. Paul Cowan was a journalist who threw himself into situations that might just change his mind, and how many of us dare to do that? In the deeply humanizing portrait of illegal aliens, he notes how "I'd always included *braceros*"—Mexicans who traveled back and forth on legally sanctioned work contracts—"in my private litany of the oppressed." Instead, he found "they talked nostalgically, not bitterly, about their adventures" north of the border. He calls the chapter "Still the Promised Land"—a self-reproach to someone who once proudly called himself an "un-American." In a profile of Jesse Jackson, he encounters a man on the verge of apostasy from the left: Jackson, who was then deeply opposed to abortion, was the keynoter at the 1978 meeting of the Republican National Committee. Cowan sat and listened, relegating his own voice to the background. That quiet and reflective voice may account for a mystery regarding Cowan, whom I had never heard of at all when I encountered this book by accident last year. Flashier contemporaries went on to greater fame. Cowan's willingness to play down his own ego—indeed, to mock his own ego—accounts for some of his obscurity.

The more famous names often seemed more macho; there is something about the male journalist and the trope of physical courage. Though Cowan was no chicken: covering a nationwide transportation strike, he thumbs a ride with a trucker through Ohio, where strike supporters are shooting scabs from overpasses. But then comes the characteristic Cowan move: the introduction of a discordant image. He describes a group of college students goofing around in a truck stop's game room, himself "oddly envious, as they chatted cozily about the plays they planned to see during a weekend in New York." He would rather be with them. It is a meditation on a deeper meaning of courage. What journalist, reporting a story, forcing yourself on strangers, attempting to convince yourself that you have something worth saying about a world not your own, hasn't felt the desire to be somewhere else—anywhere else? And what, really, is more difficult: admitting that to yourself (and the world: Cowan wrote of his "fear that I'll appear a fool"), or placing yourself in the way of a "dangerous" situation that renders moot the question of whether what you're doing is worth writing about? The latter course is a way to banish the real fear. Sometimes you realize, reading *The Tribes of America*, that physical courage and psychic courage are inversely proportional.

The book is not just a collection of published articles. Cowan revised and extended the articles by revisiting the places he'd reported on. You want scary? Imagine catching up with the people you originally thought you'd turned into heroes with your stories, and who you now know think you've sold them out.

In 1974 Cowan was among the onslaught of outsiders—students, politicians, scribblers, filmmakers—who descended on Harlan County, Kentucky, to chronicle a coal miners' strike. He arrived bearing fantasies. The locale was legendary: "Bloody Harlan," site of the depression-era strike that inspired the song "Which Side Are You On?" "Some of the journalists I admired most—Theodore Dreiser, Sherwood Anderson, and John Dos Passos—had been part of a committee that investigated working conditions in Harlan in 1931," Cowan explained. They had left as heroes, or so he thought. Why couldn't he? He overlooked the arrogance of some of those earlier reformers, who had distributed copies of the *Daily Worker* to miners and then stood by as those very possessors of the *Daily Worker* were removed to jails in remote hamlets reachable only by mule. In Harlan, Cowan partnered with a young miner with leadership ambitions, Jerry Johnson, who seemed more cosmopolitan than all the rest: "I began to fantasize that we were a latter-day version of Butch Cassidy and the Sundance Kid, pledged to cleanse the mining town of its heritage of corruption." Sure, some of Jerry's values were different, such as his devotion to the land and his traditional marriage. His motivations were different too. Jerry was moved less by abstractions of justice than by a passion to recover the folkways of his ancestors' Appalachia before it was commandeered by the greedy overlords of coal. Cowan, the left-wing universalist, emphasized their commonality and romanticized the differences. "I began to think of them as the lost tribe of the working class," he wrote of the miners—arrogating himself, dangerously, a role as their anthropologist.

It couldn't end well.

Jerry hated the story that was meant to lionize him and ended up hating its author too—who Jerry thought had rendered Harlan's traditionalism in the *Voice* as titillating local color incidental to the political struggle, when to many in Harlan their traditions as they understood them were the point of the political struggle. Only upon returning did Cowan realize that these friendly people "felt a smoldering resentment toward outsiders"—even, or especially, outsiders who parachuted in and styled themselves as saviors. He had made a terrible botch of things. "Harlan County: The Power and the Shame," he titled this chapter. Part of that shame, he suggested, was his own. He had "indicated a set of commitments—and an unquestioning acceptance of Jerry's view of the strike—that my articles didn't really reflect."

That, he says, "helped me distill the argument that was the genesis of this book": that the passions of reformers can sometimes betray a contempt for the common sense of ordinary people, leading in turn to a dangerous narcissism that could transform someone like him into a close kin of those arrogant school bureaucrats in West Virginia.

Cowan reckoned with that danger most explicitly in his book's concluding chapter. In 1972 "the urban journalistic and political elite"—a tribe in its own right—had flooded another parochial locale, the Middle District of Pennsylvania, where Richard Nixon's Justice Department had staged a politically motivated conspiracy trial designed to neutralize the bands of Catholic radicals trying to end the war in Vietnam by disrupting the draft system. Cowan's tribe came with "visions of jurors lifted from the pages of Sinclair Lewis's *Main Street*." So did the tribe of John Mitchell, Nixon's attorney general, whose Justice Department was counting on these terrified Silent Majoritarians to sentence the defendants to an eternity underneath the jail.

Well, the yokels saw that the government's case was patently absurd, so the yokels had no trouble acquitting. "How stupid did those people in Washington think we were?" one juror later asked Cowan.

That was how Cowan ended the book. The Harrisburg experience, he concludes, "left me feeling that my attitudes toward that group of Americans (like the attitudes of most lawyers, reporters, and defendants—members of the urban elite who were connected to the case) were just as narrow and parochial as their attitudes toward us." He vowed to do better.

By the time I read that, around Christmas in 2003, I had an aching question I wanted to ask Paul Cowan. I wanted to know what had become of him ideologically. After all, in the mid-1970s, other writers were also raising criticisms about the urban journalistic and political elite and their self-serving condescension toward "heartland" people and their values. These writers were also discovering a newfound "respect for the stability of religion, of ceremony, of family life." They recognized the habits of a former radicalism as a set of blinds, just as Cowan had, and embraced what Cowan called "the more primal part of oneself" and the conviction—as Cowan wrote—that "cultures aren't clay that you can sculpt to your liking." These writers called themselves neoconservatives. Had Paul Cowan become one of them?

I couldn't ask him that question; he died of cancer in 1988. So I called Paul's widow, Rachel, his frequent companion in many of these chapters. What Rachel Cowan told me was that her husband was just as proud to write from the left at the end as he was at the beginning. He continued to work for *The Village Voice*; one of his last big stories was a profile of the victims of the Three Mile Island nuclear accident, also in the Middle District of Pennsylvania.

Politically, the answer made sense to me. It shows in Paul Cowan's ultimate judgments—for example, that the border guards whom he also deeply humanized in his portrait of illegal aliens, otherwise decent men and professionals, ultimately suffered from a racist inability to recognize the full humanity of the "wets" they hunted. It shows in his conclusion to the West Virginia chapter, in which he faces a moment of truth with the Creekers' charismatic leader: he has to grant her point that "maybe there is no school system that can provide for your kids and mine," but concludes, "I would like to think there is room for fundamentalists in my America. But I'm not sure there is room for me in theirs."

The answer also made sense to me as someone on the hunt for good writing. His ability to probe where those he disagreed with were coming from while still understanding why he disagreed with them—he knows which side he's on—was a token of his moral seriousness and his comfort with moral complexity. He was equally allergic to moral relativism as to moral dogma, which is exactly what made him a great journalist. I came to this realization while thinking of another book published in 1979. It was written by a bad journalist, who in his previous book had proved himself to be a very good one. That previous book was called *Making It*, and its descriptions of subterranean social forces that no one had described before—in this case, those shaping the New York literary world—were in their way as astonishing as the journalism in Cowan's *The Tribes of America*. But Norman Podhoretz's next book, *Breaking Ranks: A Political Memoir*, one of the most famous and influential books of neoconservatism, was a very lame one. Podhoretz told "the whole story of how and why I went from being a liberal to being a radical and then finally to being an enemy of radicalism in all its forms and varieties." Podhoretz had picked the wrong side. So he rejected it root and branch, right down to its core principle, social solidarity. The Republican-style "politics of interest," he wrote, was "the only antidote to the plague" of sixties radicalism.

You can agree or disagree with the politics. I think it's hard to disagree that Podhoretz became a much worse writer, much less skilled at describing the world. In *Making It*, self-examination was the taproot of social observation. In *Breaking Ranks*—and his subsequent work—Podhoretz recognized only demons that existed outside himself. The left left him; he always stayed the same. Podhoretz claimed a moral courage that was inversely proportional to his actual courage, which was sorely lacking. For perhaps it wasn't the left that was dogmatic, but himself—and dogmatists make terrible journalists.

Paul Cowan took a different course, and that is the meaning of his work. He looked inside himself. He found sins—his own sins, not the sins of some abstraction called "the left," to be rejected as such—and he reckoned with them. Which is hard work. He tested his prejudices against reality, about as deeply as anyone could test them; he embraced new principles, cleaving to the ones worth keeping. He saw virtues in bourgeois virtue. But that didn't paralyze his conscience. He saw that America had tribes, and that the left-leaning Ivy League professionalism he inhabited was one of them, with its own characteristic inanities. That wasn't the end of the story for Cowan, but rather a new, richer beginning.

Nicholson Baker

DANIEL DEFOE'S
A JOURNAL OF THE PLAGUE YEAR

I first read Daniel Defoe's *A Journal of the Plague Year* on a train from Boston to New York. That's the truth. It's not a very interesting truth, but it's true. I could say that I first read it sitting on a low green couch in the old smoking room of the Cincinnati Palladium, across from a rather glum-looking Henry Kissinger. Or that I found a beat-up Longman's 1895 edition of Defoe's *Plague Year* in a dumpster near the Recycle-a-Bicycle shop on Pearl Street when I was high on Guinness and roxies, and I opened it and was drawn into its singular, fearful world, and I sat right down in my own vomit and read the book straight through. It would be easy for me to say these things. But if I did, I would be inventing—and, as John Hersey wrote, the sacred rule for the journalist (or the memoirist, or indeed for any nonfiction writer) is: Never Invent.

That's what makes Daniel Defoe, the founder of English journalism, such a thorny shrub. The hoaxers and the embellishers, the fake autobiographers, look on Defoe as a kind of patron saint. Defoe lied a lot. But he also hated his lying habit, at least sometimes. He said the lying made a hole in the heart. About certain events he wanted truth told. And one event he really cared about was the great plague of 1665, which happened when he was about five years old.

A Journal of the Plague Year begins quietly, without any apparatus of learnedness. It doesn't try to connect this recent plague with past plagues. It draws no historical or classical or literary parallels. It just begins: "It was about the beginning of September, 1664, that I, among the rest of my neighbors, heard in ordinary discourse that the plague was returned again in Holland." The "I" is not Defoe, but an older proxy, somebody mysteriously named H. F., who says he is a saddler. H. F. lives halfway between Aldgate Church and Whitechapel, "on the left hand or north side of the street." That's all we know about him.

H. F. watches the bills of mortality mount—he keeps track—and he debates with himself whether to stay in town or flee. His brother tells him to save himself, get away. But no, H. F. decides to stay. He listens. He walks around. He sees a man race out of an alley, apparently singing and making clownish gestures, pursued by women and children—surgeons had been at work on his plague sores. "By laying strong caustics on them, the surgeons had, it seems, hopes to break them—which caustics were then upon him, burning his flesh as with a hot iron." H. F. hears screams—many different kinds of screams, and screeches, and shrieks. In an empty street in Lothbury, a window opens suddenly just over his head. "A woman gave three frightful screeches, and then cried, 'Oh! death, death, death!'" There was no other movement. The street was still. "For people had no curiosity now in any case."

At the plague's height, H. F. writes, there were no funerals, no wearing of black, no tolling bells, no coffins. "Whole streets seemed to be desolated," he says, and "doors were left open, windows stood shattering with the wind in empty houses for want of people to shut them. In a word, people began to give up themselves to their fears and to think that all regulations and methods were in vain, and that there was nothing to be hoped for but an universal desolation."

* * *

What do we know about Defoe? Very little. He was one of the most prolific men ever to lift a pen, but he wrote almost nothing about himself. Not many letters have survived. Readers have been attributing and de-attributing Defoe's anonymous journalism ever since he died, broke, in Ropemaker's Alley, in 1731. He was almost always writing about someone else—or pretending to be someone else. There are a few engravings of him, and only one surviving prose description. It's unfriendly—in fact, it was a sort of warrant for his arrest, printed in a newspaper when Defoe was wanted by the government on a charge of seditious libel. "He is a middle-sized, spare man," said the description, "about forty years old, of a brown complexion, and dark brown-colored hair, but wears a wig; a hooked nose, a sharp chin, grey eyes, and a large mole near his mouth." Anyone who could furnish information leading to his apprehension by Her Majesty's justices of the peace, said the notice, would receive a reward of fifty pounds.

We know that Defoe, late in life, wrote the first English novels—*Robinson Crusoe* in 1719, about a lonely sailor who sees a man's naked footprint on the beach, and *Moll Flanders* in 1722, about a woman who was "twelve year a whore." We know that he was born about 1660, the son of a London butcher or candlemaker named James Foe. In his twenties, Daniel went into business as a hosier—that is, as a seller of women's stockings. Trade and speculation went well for a while, then less well, and then he had to hide from his creditors, to whom he owed seventeen thousand pounds. He was rescued by friends on high, and began writing pamphlets and poetry.

Soon he was running a large company that made roofing tiles—and the pamphleteering was surprisingly successful. He added a Frenchifying "de" to his name. In 1701 he produced the most-selling poem up to that time, "The True-Born Englishman," which hymned his native land as a motley nation of immigrants: "Thus, from a mixture of all kinds began / That het'rogenous thing, an Englishman." Another pamphlet—in which, several decades before Swift's "Modest Proposal," he pretended to be a rabid high-churchman who advocated the deportation or hanging of nonconformists—got him clamped in a pillory in 1703 and sent to Newgate Prison.

While in prison he started a newspaper, the *Review*, an antecedent to *The Tatler* and *The Spectator*, which Richard Steele and Joseph Addison would launch within a decade. Besides essays and opinion pieces, the *Review* had an early advice column, and a "weekly history of Nonsense, Impertinence, Vice, and Debauchery." That same year, still in prison, he gathered intelligence on a disaster that had visited parts of England. His book, *The Storm*—about what he called "the greatest and the longest storm that ever the world saw"—is one of the earliest extended journalistic narratives in English.

For a faker, Defoe had an enormous appetite for truth and life and bloody specificity. He wanted to know everything knowable about trade, about royalty, about lowlife, about the customs of other countries, about ships, about folk remedies and quack doctors, about disasters, about scientific advances, and about the shops and streets of London. He listened to stories people told him. "In this way of Talk I was always upon the Inquiry," one of his characters says, "asking Questions of things done in Publick, as well as in Private." But his desire to impersonate and playact kept surging up and getting him into trouble. He wanted to pass as someone he wasn't—as a French diplomat, as a Turkish spy, as a fallen woman, as a person who'd seen a ghost, as a pre-Dickensian pickpocket.

He was an especially industrious first-person crime writer. Once he ghostwrote the story of a thief and jailbreaker named Jack Sheppard. To promote its publication, Defoe had Sheppard pause at the gallows and, before a huge crowd, hand out the freshly printed pamphlets as his last testament—or so the story goes. "The rapidity with which this book sold is probably unparalleled," writes an early biographer, William Lee.

Robinson Crusoe is Defoe's most famous hoax. We describe it as a novel, of course, but it wasn't born that way. On its 1719 title page, the book was billed as the strange, surprising adventures of a mariner who lived all alone for eight-and-twenty years on an uninhabited island, "Written by H I M S E L F"—and people at first took this claim for truth and bought thousands of copies. This prompted an enemy satirist, Charles Gildon, to rush out a pamphlet, "The Life and Strange Surprising Adventures of Daniel de Foe, Formerly of London, Hosier, Who has lived above fifty Years all alone by himself, in the Kingdoms of North and South Britain."

Addison called Defoe "a false, shuffling, prevaricating rascal." Another contemporary said he was a master of "forging a story and imposing it on the world as truth." One of Defoe's nineteenth-century biographers, William Minto, wrote: "He was a great, a truly great liar, perhaps the greatest liar that ever lived."

And yet that's not wholly fair. A number of the things that people later took to be Defoe's dazzlingly colorful tapestries of fabrication, weren't. In 1718, in *Mist's Journal*, Defoe gave a detailed account of the volcanic explosion of the island of St. Vincent, relying, he said, on letters he had received about it. A century passed, and doubts crept in. One Defoe scholar said that the St. Vincent story was imaginary; a second said it was tomfoolery; a third said it was "make-believe" and "entirely of Defoe's invention." But the island of St. Vincent had actually blown up, and it had made a lot of noise as it blew. Defoe had done his journalistic best to report this prodigy.

Something similar happened in the case of *A Journal of the Plague Year*. When Defoe published it, he (as usual) left himself off the title page, ascribing the story to H. F. "Written by a Citizen," the title page falsely, sales-boostingly claimed, "Who Continued All the While in London." People believed that for a while; but by 1780, at least, it was generally known that Defoe was the book's author. Then someone did some arithmetic and realized that Defoe had been a young child when the plague struck London—whereupon they began calling the book a historical novel, unequaled in vividness and circumstantiality. Walter Raleigh, in his late nineteenth-century history of the English novel, called the book "sham history." In a study of "pseudofactual" fiction, Barbara Foley says the *Plague Year* "creates the majority of its particulars." And John Hollowell, investigating the literary origins of the New Journalism, writes that Defoe's book is "fiction masquerading as fact." Is it?

* * *

One night H. F. visits the forty-foot burial trench in Aldgate churchyard, near where he lives. "A terrible pit it was," he writes, "and I could not resist my curiosity to go and see it." He watches the dead cart dip and the bodies fall "promiscuously" into the pit, while a father stands silently by. Then the father, beside himself with grief, suddenly lets out a cry. Another time, H. F. describes the butcher's market. "People used all possible precaution," he says. "When any one bought a joint of meat in the market, they would not take it out of the butcher's hand, but took it off the hooks themselves. On the other hand, the butcher would not touch the money, but have it put into a pot full of vinegar, which he kept for that purpose."

A Journal of the Plague Year is an astounding performance. It's shocking, it's messy, it's moving, it sobs aloud with its losses, it's got all the urgency and loopingly prolix insistence of a man of sympathy who has lived through an urban catastrophe and wants to tell you what it was like. The fear of death, notes H. F., "took away all bowels of love, all concern for one another." But not universally: "There were many instances of immovable affection, pity and duty." And Defoe's narrator is at pains to discount some of the stories that he hears. He is told, for example, of nurses smothering plague victims with wet cloths to hasten their end. But the details are suspiciously unvarying, and in every version, no matter where he encounters it, the event is said to have happened on the opposite side of town. There is, H. F. judges, "more of tale than of truth" in these accounts.

Still, there's the false frame. The story isn't really being told by H. F., it's being told by Defoe. That's clearly a forgery—although more understandable when you learn that Defoe had an uncle with those initials, Henry Foe. Henry was in fact a saddler, who lived in Aldgate near the burial pit. It seems that in order to launch himself into the telling of this overwhelmingly complex story of London's ordeal, Defoe needed to think and write in his uncle's voice. The "I" is more than a bit of commercial-minded artifice. The ventriloquism, the fictional first-person premise, helped Defoe to unspool and make sequential sense of what he knew. He sifted through and used a mass of contemporary published sources, as any journalist would, and he enlivened that printed store with anecdotes that people had told him over the years. (His father could have been a source for the butcher's vinegar pot.) The book feels like something heartfelt, that grew out of decades of accumulated notes and memories—although written with impressive speed. It doesn't feel like an artificial swizzle of falsifications.

In 1919, a young scholar, Watson Nicholson, wrote a book on the sources of Defoe's *Journal of the Plague Year*. He was quite upset by the notion that the *Journal* was now, without qualification, being called a novel. In his book, Nicholson claimed to have established "overwhelming evidence of the complete authenticity of Defoe's 'masterpiece of the imagination.'" There was not, Nicholson said, "a single essential statement in the *Journal* not based on historic fact." True, Defoe had a way of embroidering, but even so, "the employment of the first person in the narrative in no sense interferes with the authenticity of the facts recorded."

Other critics agreed. In 1965, Frank Bastian checked what Defoe said in the *Journal* against Pepys's *Diary*, which Defoe couldn't have seen because it wasn't decoded until a century later. "Characters and incidents once confidently asserted to be the products of Defoe's fertile imagination," wrote Bastian, "repeatedly prove to have been factual." Introducing the Penguin edition of the *Plague Year* in 1966, Anthony Burgess wrote: "Defoe was our first great novelist because he was our first great journalist."

Six thousand people a month died in London's plague, most of them poor. The locations of many burial pits passed from memory. One was later used, according to Defoe, as a "yard for keeping hogs"; another was rediscovered when the foundation of a grand house was being dug: "The women's sculls were quite distinguished by their long hair." Is the author being a reporter here, or a novelist? We don't know. We want to know.

Daniel Defoe seems to have needed a pocket full of passports to get where he was going. But the moral of his story, at least for the nonfictionist, still is: Never Invent. People love hoaxes in theory—from a distance—but they also hate being tricked. If you make up sad things and insist that they're true, nobody afterward will fully trust what you write.

15

Dale Maharidge

⸻

JAMES AGEE'S
LET US NOW PRAISE FAMOUS MEN

Some years ago I dined at the Harvard Lampoon, the closed society that publishes the eponymous humor magazine. Located in a castle funded in part by William Randolph Hearst, the Lampoon's chambers harbor myriad relics: a medieval clock, a fourth-century stained-glass window, a conquistador's armor, a couch from San Simeon, altars of worship to writers such as James Agee. It was because of my relationship with *Let Us Now Praise Famous Men*, Agee and Walker Evans's collaborative work about Alabama sharecroppers during the Great Depression, that I'd been invited to socialize at the castle.

There was no electric light. Dozens of candles illuminated the rooms. My host, the Lampoon president, sat in a throne six feet tall and four feet wide at the head of a long table. Dinner was served promptly at ten. Conversation was formal and strange jazz filled the air. I was astonished when, at meal's end, a man flung his plate to the floor. Suddenly there was a cacophony of crashing plates, spraying shards of porcelain; noodles hung from a coat of arms. Two men jumped atop the table and kicked off the remaining plates. My host assured me this was normal. The china was broken every night.

"Who cleans up the mess?"

"We certainly don't. We hire help, servants. The Lampoon has more money than most colleges."

I was further astonished when men wearing ties attacked the piano with feet, fists, and chairs. The splintering of wood rose over the techno beat of the song, "Pump Up the Volume." The piano was old and a fresh one was being delivered the next day.

Amid this display, Lampoon members besieged me with questions about Agee, hanging on my words. They talked admiringly of Agee's exploits in the Combat Zone, Boston's red-light district. The piano was now a heap of waste. Men stood smoking, sated. A woman cavorted in the rubble in a ghostly dance out of sync with the throbbing music. I flung my beer bottle against a wall; it exploded in a shower of glass. I fled and wandered the frozen streets of Cambridge, Agee on my mind.

Agee affects those who read him. For Jimmy Carter, whom I met in Nashville in 1989, the impact of *Let Us Now Praise Famous Men* seemed to be moral and religious. For Tad Mosel, whom I met at the seventy-fifth Pulitzer Prize anniversary party in 1991, Agee's presence was supernatural. Mosel's 1961 Pulitzer-winning play, *All the Way Home*, was adapted from Agee's posthumously published novel, *A Death in the Family.* "I talked with him and asked him to forgive me when I changed things," Mosel said of communicating with Agee's spirit. "I talked with him for two years. Did he talk with you?"

Agee talks to me, but not as he did to Mosel or Carter, and certainly not as he does to the Lampoon members, who represent an extreme wing of a de facto Agee cult (Agee wrote for the *Lampoon* while at Harvard). Agee literally informs *And Their Children After Them* (1989), the book in which the photographer Michael Williamson and I documented the lives of the survivors and descendants of the three families with whom Agee lived in Alabama. We brought forward their story and the meaning of poverty and its fallout a half-century later.

Agee has informed my other books in a less topical but equally vital way. Joe Elbert, assistant managing editor for photography at *The Washington Post* (and Michael Williamson's boss), likes to give speeches excoriating editors, both print and photo, for not taking risks. Elbert doesn't edit conventionally, as in judging a photo on technical points. He considers how an image makes him *feel*. For what it takes to get this result, in photos or words, I always look to Agee. His was not cold, buttoned-down, dispassionate reportage. It was about danger, getting hot and sweaty, getting close, close enough to hurt, to feel something, to say something.

This is not a review of *Let Us Now Praise Famous Men*, which is indescribable anyway. One must read it. But be forewarned: it's uneven. Parts are, frankly, boring. But most of it captivates. The sum of the whole is well worth the journey. Instead, I want to delve into Agee's journalistic process, a way of working that transcends his book. Agee embodies passion and soul, two qualities that some editors fear because they mistakenly equate them with bias, or having an agenda when covering the human side of social issues. Agee was not about doing journalism. He was about living it. This secret can be applied to book journalism, alternative weeklies, and even daily newspapers, though one must be stealthful with the latter. Agee described himself and Evans as "spies." If one works for a passion-hating city editor, it's imperative to think and act like a spy.

* * *

Agee was a poet before he was a spy. When he was twenty-five a book of his verse was published by Yale University Press. In 1932 the poet went straight from his Harvard graduation ceremony to Henry Luce's two-year-old *Fortune* magazine. Jobs were scarce, and Luce had been impressed by a spoof issue of *Time* that Agee had edited his senior year. The only reason Agee fit in at all at *Fortune* was the backdrop of the Great Depression—instead of solely glorifying wealth, Luce knew he had to publish sociological articles about the New Deal.

Agee found himself stuck in the middle level of Luce's editorial assembly line, churning out his share of "mind-numbing assignments," according to his biographer, Laurence Bergreen. Yet he sometimes produced profound journalism—on the Tennessee Valley Authority, industrial smoke, the American roadside. He wrote at night in the Chrysler Building, fifty-two floors above Manhattan's streets, blasting Beethoven on a portable record player, alone.

By 1935 he was languishing, and his work troubles flowed into his marriage. He wanted to reach heights with his writing but felt he was stumbling. He was disgusted with his bosses—even then, editors feared passion—and went so far as to talk with his colleagues about a fantasy of shooting Luce dead.

"Who, what, where, when and why (or how) is the primal cliché and complacency of journalism," Agee wrote in *Let Us Now Praise Famous Men*. Because of how journalism was practiced, it was difficult to get at truth. Could journalism be blamed, he wrote, any more than a cow be blamed "for not being a horse?" Yes. "The difference is, and the reason one can respect or anyhow approve of the cow, that few cows can have the delusion or even the desire to be horses, and that none of them could get away with it even with a small part of the public. The very blood and semen of journalism, on the contrary, is a broad and successful form of lying. Remove that form of lying and you no longer have journalism."

He went on leave to Florida for six months in a failed attempt to save his marriage. He was adrift, proof that one's personal life is intertwined with the professional. He returned in 1936 to an assignment from *Fortune*'s managing editor: travel with Walker Evans to the South for a piece on the nine million cotton sharecroppers, the most hardscrabble poor in the nation.

The stakes were high as Agee and Evans hit the road that June. Agee's life, personal and professional, became wrapped up in the assignment. He could not fail. The pair cast about and found three families—the Woods, Gudgers, and Ricketts—on Hobe's Hill, a bleak plateau south of Tuscaloosa, Alabama.

After a month Agee had a story, but it was a cow masquerading as a horse. He left Evans in a Birmingham hotel and drove off in aimless despair, contemplating a roadside hooker whom he passed up, then a fight at a lunch counter likewise avoided. He ended up back on Hobe's Hill. A storm hit. George Gudger invited him to stay the night in the family's shotgun shack. Agee graciously declined, then hated himself for doing so as he drove down the mud-slick road. He had to get closer to the family, and he'd blown his chance. Then, either by accident or on purpose—Agee himself did not know—his car crashed into a ditch. He rolled up his pants and walked back to the Gudgers', where he lived for three weeks.

This is when Agee discovered the horse.

When he came home from Alabama in September, however, Luce had turned rightward from being a New Deal moderate. Sociological articles were out, and Agee and Evans's story was rejected. They decided to publish a book; to hell with Luce. Published in 1941 in a country mobilizing for war, the book was a commercial flop. Agee went on to make a name as a movie reviewer for *Time* and *The Nation*. He lived hard, drinking and smoking and womanizing, dying of a heart attack in a Manhattan taxi in

1955. He was forty-five. In 1958, *A Death in the Family* was awarded a Pulitzer Prize. In 1960, *Let Us Now Praise Famous Men* was reissued, racking up serious sales.

* * *

In 1982 I was given a copy of *Let Us Now Praise Famous Men* by Diane Alters, a writer/editor colleague at *The Sacramento Bee*. Michael Williamson (another *Bee* colleague) and I were embarking upon our first book, *Journey to Nowhere*, about the new homeless, and Diane wanted me to read Agee for inspiration.

The first time Agee affected how I approach my work was in Houston in 1983, when Michael and I met Jim and Bonnie Alexander and their two kids. Jim was a job-seeking welder, and the family ended up living in a tent. We set up camp next to them, living out of our car. We shared meals, played pool with Jim, got drunk, talked by campfire. On night six Jim showed us his pistol. Bonnie told about a dinner when there was just one potato. "Boy, I sliced it real thin," she said. "I'm never going to let that happen again," Jim said. "First, I'll go hunting for food. If that doesn't work, I hit a 7-Eleven. I won't take money. But I'll take food. My kids won't starve."

We wouldn't have achieved this degree of intimacy had we not lived with the family. This was relatively simple. Things were stunningly more complicated when Michael and I went to Alabama in 1985 to find the 128 survivors and offspring of the original 22 family members from *Let Us Now Praise Famous Men*. They were no longer sharecropping—machines had ended that—but most were still at the bottom of the socioeconomic order. We unearthed a deeper lesson from Agee as we spent three years on the story.

We didn't literally move in with any of the descendants, but we emotionally set up house. We were invested to the core of our beings in the lives of those we were documenting. We didn't set out to do this. It just happened. It mattered not if our work never materialized into a book—for three years publishers rejected us. I had $12,000 of my savings in the project. When things looked most hopeless, Michael spent $1,500 he didn't have on a trip, for one photo. We had to journey to a conclusion even if the story remained dormant in the notebooks and film negatives stored in our garages. It was personal.

Agee was a strong influence on the New Journalism of the 1960s, his biographer Bergreen and others have noted. While some laud Agee, others trash him. Many critics of New Journalism and some who attempt its practice but fail miss a vital point about Agee's work. It was not really about "style," nor how Agee used the first person. Yes, Agee was a stylist, and he wasn't shy about using an "I." But these aspects are incidental to his journalism. More important was that Agee emotionally connected with the families. In order to get their stories, he gave of himself. He confronted the wall of "objectivity," of not getting close to one's subjects, and smashed through it.

This brand of reporting is akin to "Method acting," in which actors take on the persona of the characters they are portraying. With journalism this means total immersion—method reporting. It started that day Agee showed up at the Gudgers' door, mud-caked, his car wrecked in a ditch. Earlier that afternoon during the storm, when he took refuge with the family in their shack, he focused on the eyes of ten-year-old Maggie Louise Gudger, "temperatureless, keen, serene and wise and pure gray eyes." Looking into them, he wrote, was "scary as hell, and even more mysterious than frightening."

In the coming weeks he watched the family picking cotton. He took Maggie on rides through the county, told her about life in the big city. She was smart, and he saw in the girl hope for breaking out of the cycle of poverty. One night he perched her on the chicken coop, beneath the starry sky. Maggie wondered about her future. Agee later wrote that she might get her wish, and become a nurse or a teacher.

We were left with Maggie's hopes in *Let Us Now Praise Famous Men*. I found that she sharecropped until her second husband died in 1958, then became a waitress, raising her four children. Maggie descended into alcoholism and depression. She moved back home. One day in 1971 she stopped in a store to buy a bottle of something while her sister waited in the car. At home later the sister heard a thud. Rushing into the room, the sister saw the empty bottle whose contents had just been swallowed by Maggie. It was rat poison. The family tried to force saltwater down her throat, to make her expel it, but she clenched her teeth.

"I don't wanna live," Maggie said. "I wanna die. I've took all I can take."

In *And Their Children After Them* I wrote, "They buried Maggie Louise at the edge of a hill, two miles up the road from where she had sat on the chicken coop that night and dreamed the stars."

I needed to see, feel, and smell everything connected to Maggie Louise, including Agee. Michael and I spent two days, sometimes on hands and knees, in a chigger-infested jungle of pine and kudzu seeking vestiges of the Gudger shack. I tracked Agee in New York City, through his daughter, ex-wife, friends; at Harvard, at the *Lampoon*. I obtained Maggie's suicide note and found her children, and we got to know some of them with an intensity that cannot be addressed here in any form that would do justice to the story.

There's no guidebook for this kind of work. It's about being human first, a journalist second. One has to submit to a story for which one has passion, and allow life to happen. The story does not exactly write itself; it is *journalisme verité*.

* * *

Let Us Now Praise Famous Men was a bitter disappointment for Agee, "like a dead child," a friend of Agee's had told me, not to be discussed. He felt like a failure, and this led to increased drinking and smoking.

Did something happen in the South that darkly affected Agee as his life spiraled to its early end? He never again did a project like that book. Perhaps he'd said all he'd needed to through this form of work, abandoning it just as he'd left poetry behind. Or possibly it was the children from two marriages he had to support and the impossibility of earning a living from this kind of journalism. Or maybe it was simply too emotionally costly. He turned in new directions, plunging into Hollywood. He wrote the screenplay for John Huston's *African Queen*, and biographer Bergreen notes that we see Agee in the brooding and boozing loner played by Humphrey Bogart.

My editor asked me if method journalism had affected me. It's a question that immediately raises another: How can one boil down into a few paragraphs the weight of the work's emotion, without sounding self-absorbed or silly? But there are deeper reasons, whose nature is possibly not fully acknowledged to myself, for wanting to avoid the question of effects. I liken it to the cessation of a long-term romantic relationship. One moves on, yet the pains and joys remain below the surface for years and cannot really be discussed. Denial can rule. There's a danger in method reporting, outside any discussion about journalism. One does not walk away unscathed.

For years I continued to brush against the darkness of Agee's life—there were other intense experiences beyond the Lampoon dinner—and he became a mirror as I figured some things out, and learned the most important lesson from him. Agee is evidence that one can be too serious, too self-absorbed. It's vital to step back from this kind of work. It's one reason that I own an off-the-grid house on the Pacific Coast where I live part of the year and tend tomato plants and haul firewood.

Does this kind of journalism take a toll on those written about? We can look to Agee and Maggie Louise for some insight.

"Good God, if I have caused you any harm in this," Agee wrote about Maggie Louise in *Let Us Now Praise Famous Men*, "if I have started within you any harmful change . . . forgive me if you can, despise me if you must."

Maggie Louise didn't read this until not long before she killed herself, family members told me, for Agee never sent them books and they didn't learn *Let Us Now Praise Famous Men* existed until the 1960s. Was it a cruel reminder, after a life hard-lived, of her unrealized dreams? Her aunt and son said she never gave up her affection for Agee; she didn't seem outwardly upset.

Who really knows about any of this? What is certain is that Agee, the urbane writer from Harvard, a poet and Hollywood celebrity, and Maggie Louise Gudger, sharecropper and waitress, lived weirdly parallel lives. Maggie chose a direct path to her end; Agee's was less direct but equally willed, by hard drinking and ignoring his doctors. As I wrote in *Children*, "They were both dreamers and, deep down, tragic people who yearned for something they could not define even as they came to know finally that it had irretrievably escaped them. They died, though far apart in years and miles, at the same age—at forty-five—as if defining a limit for the number of years of failed dreams a dreamer can be asked to endure."

Robert Lipsyte

——

PAUL GALLICO'S
FAREWELL TO SPORT

In 1938, the year I was born, Paul Gallico published his valedictory *Farewell to Sport*, a thoughtful meditation on the "wildest, maddest, and most glamorous period in all the history of sport," which just happened to coincide with his fourteen years as a New York *Daily News* sportswriter. Gallico was no mere press-box pundit. Long before the late George Plimpton's showy turns as quarterback, pitcher, and boxer, Gallico pioneered participatory sports journalism. He swam with Johnny Weismuller, golfed with Bobby Jones, and lasted less than two minutes in the ring with Jack Dempsey.

I was about fifteen when I first read the book and readily absorbed its Galliconian pronouncements, such as "like all people who spring from what we call low origins, [Babe] Ruth never had any inhibitions"; Mildred (Babe) Didrikson Zaharias became one of the greatest athletes of the century "simply because she would not or could not compete with women at their own and best game—man-snatching. It was an escape, a compensation. She would beat them at everything else they tried to do"; and the reason basketball "appeals to the Hebrew . . . is that the game places a premium on an alert, scheming mind and flashy trickiness, artful dodging and general smart aleckness."

Even as a Hebrew without much game, I was swept along by Gallico's confidence. He had a cool and cocky style leavened with just enough Great Books references to connect a young 1950s smart aleck to the elitism, sexism, and faux macho of the 1930s sportswriters who had dipped their noses as well as their pens in other men's testosterone. I felt manlier through his access to the Manassa Mauler, the Brown Bomber, the Iron Horse. And his dismissal of women athletes was reassuring; if a girl did manage to whip you, it was only because she was likely not truly female. Boys in my day were labeled "girls" and "fags" if they didn't at least pay lip service to the emerging values of what I now call Jock Culture, that stew of honor, self-absorption, generosity, greed, bravery, emotional constriction, tenderness, domination, and defiance that commands so much of our national life.

I was, however, slightly uncomfortable with Gallico's remarks about the "colored brother" who is "not nearly so sensible to pain as his white brother. He has a thick, hard skull and good hands." It smacked of racism; my parents worked in black neighborhoods, and I knew better. But I was willing to give Gallico the same pass that most of my textbooks gave the slave-owning Thomas Jefferson. Gallico too was a man of his times. After all, he had written *Farewell* a decade before Jackie Robinson.

Four years after I read the book, still a teenager, I landed in the sports department of *The New York Times*. I'd answered an ad for what I considered would be only a summer job before heading west to write books and movies, just like Gallico. But as much as I hated being a copyboy, I stayed on past that summer because I dreamed that someday, I too might be "at the tennis tournament at Forest Hills . . . drinking an ice tea . . . surrounded by beautifully dressed women and soft-spoken men in summer flannels," and the next day be "in a frowsy, ribald fight camp, gagging over a glass of needle beer," where I'd find "doubtful blondes . . . and blondes about whom there was no doubt."

Eventually I got to both places, and they were as good as Gallico had promised, especially the fight camps. As a young boxing reporter, I kept two books handy, Gallico's *Farewell* and A. J. Liebling's *The Sweet Science*, which was No. 1 on *Sports Illustrated*'s 2002 top 100 sports books of all time (*Farewell* was No. 82). Liebling was ultimately discouraging; no one else could eat and drink so much and still write so well, not to mention come up with eloquent quotes from grizzled corner men who were all but mute for me.

But Gallico was my grizzled corner man whispering into my ear. I was able to take a been-there-done-that-so-can-you message from his pages to my seat at ringside on deadline, the telegrapher at my elbow, the boxers above me, the office screaming for copy. The pressure became invigorating. To be, in his phrase, "under the guns," made writing as competitive and manly as fighting.

He also helped me understand my mixed feelings about boxing. I did love those frowzy, ribald fight camps, but never could give myself up to the fight itself. Gallico also couldn't understand how you can beat on a wounded man, and wondered if he had always been "too romantic, sentimental, and imaginative to appreciate the true hardness and grimness of what is known as the Sweet Science; perhaps I have always approached the ring from the fiction-writer's angle."

But even more important was this line: "Your circulation begins to fall off if you destroy too many illusions, especially if you yourself have created them." It helped me understand (well, sort of) why it was only after many years that I was allowed to describe Mickey Mantle—and allowed myself to describe Gallico—as anything but a noble warrior.

* * *

Gallico's background offered me supportive parallels. He too was a New Yorker, born on July 26, 1897. His father, Paolo, a composer and concert pianist, wanted Paul to follow him into music, certainly not descend into sports writing. My dad, a teacher, had similar feelings about my aspirations. Gallico went to Columbia, where he captained the varsity crew. I went to Columbia, where I quit the lightweight freshman pig boat the second time it was swamped. We both saw our futures in fiction. I don't think I would have attempted my first novel in 1967, *The Contender*, without his example. But by then I was growing away from him. I had other corner men.

While Gallico was describing Joe Louis's "sly servility," the nationally syndicated columnist Jimmy Cannon called Louis "a credit to his race, the human race," quaint now but a bold statement then. Lester Rodney, sports editor of the *Daily Worker*, was leading the struggle against sports apartheid, along with black newspapermen like Sam Lacey and Wendell Smith, who wrote for the *Baltimore Afro-American* and the *Pittsburgh Courier*, respectively. Gallico had written about Jim Crow sports and the under-the-table payments he called shamateurism, but ultimately, I thought, he was more of a cheerleader than a leader, or, to put it in his terms, more "Gee whiz" than "Oh, nuts."

In 1971, I left the *Times* to write fiction full-time. Surely my fourteen years of Ali and Cosell, Billie Jean King, Vince Lombardi, Joe Namath, the 1968 Mexico Olympics, the sneaker wars, the Socialist linebacker Dave Meggyesy, and Jim Bouton's *Ball Four* were the "wildest, maddest, and most glamorous period in all the history of sport." What was left?

I was around thirty-five when I read *Farewell to Sport* cover to cover for the second time, as research for my own 1975 valedictory, *SportsWorld: An American Dreamland*. (*Sports Illustrated* made it No. 97, calling it "an angry screed.") Now I saw Gallico as a prime example of what had been and was still wrong with sports writing: the jock-sniffing, the intellectual laziness, the moral cowardice.

What an old whore he was, always begging Babe Ruth or Gene Tunney to show up at some event he was promoting. How did that affect his coverage? His line about your circulation falling off if you destroy too many illusions began to sound like a justification of all those years he spent, to borrow a phrase of the great *Herald Tribune* sports editor Stanley Woodward, "Godding up the ball-players."

Gallico wasn't bashful about Godding up himself either. Take his line about Babe Didrikson honing her championship hurdling and jump-shooting skills to compensate for her man-snatching defeats. In his autobiography, *The Tumult and the Shouting*, the sportswriter and sportscaster Grantland Rice describes a little joke he played on his pal Gallico. During a golf match, he talked Gallico into a foot race with Didrikson, and she left him for dead. Babe tells the same story in her autobiography, *This Life I've Led*. After that race, Gallico suddenly noticed Babe's Adam's apple. Of course, if a woman beats you, she can't really be a woman.

Gallico attacked prizefighting, but never amateur boxing, because he was a founder of the Golden Gloves. And for all his big talk about how blacks were unfairly treated, he went along with the segregation of his black boxers on the road. In *Farewell*, the chapter on black athletes was called "Eightball." Nice. Was it Gallico's wishful thinking that "our next Olympic team may by natural processes have only one or two Negro stars"? In any case, he reasoned that if black athletes were used and discarded (like Jesse Owens, for example?) it was their own fault. Gallico wished that the black athlete's "racial pride carried him a few steps further than it does. His greed for the white man's blessings and the white man's mode of living defeats him and makes him a set-up for exploitation." Today, we call that "blame the victim," Paulie.

Too bad Gallico didn't stick around into my time, I thought. I would have enjoyed writing head-to-head with that bombastic fool. Then again, he probably did less harm churning out his forty-odd sentimental novels, such as *The Poseidon Adventure, The Snow Goose,* and *Mrs. 'Arris Goes to Paris.*

I wasn't paying attention when Gallico died of a heart attack on July 15, 1976, in Monaco, where he had been living with his fourth wife, the Baroness Virginia von Falz-Fein. He was seventy-eight years old. Nobody called me. I didn't know about it for years.

* * *

In 1991, my generation of copyboys took over the *Times* and invited me to join a hot new sports section under Neil Amdur. After twenty years of writing novels and screenplays and appearing on TV, I thought it might be fun to write a column again for a year or two, tops. I signed on as a contract writer so I could hold on to all my other gigs.

The column fodder of the next thirteen years—Michael Jordan, Tiger Woods, Tonya Harding, the 1998 Summer of Swat, the emergence of the woman athlete, the Gay Games, the Augusta National Golf Club, the merging of sports and entertainment, the spike in crimes by athletes— might lead some to believe we were going through the "wildest, maddest, and most glamorous period in all the history of sport." TV money fueled it and freed athletes from needing journalists to present them to the public. Athletes could control their images through ads and paid appearances. This left most sportswriters and sportscasters to choose between fawning their way into an interview with show biz-style access or making their brief, snarling encounters the story. ESPN SportsCenter's frat-boy jokiness was the most successful since it included thrilling highlights.

This time around, Jock Culture came into sharp focus for me. Right after the 1999 shootings at Columbine High School, I wrote a column suggesting that the arrogant, entitled behavior of high school athletes, encouraged by the adults who lived vicariously through their overhyped deeds, had created an everlasting divide between Jocks (and their boosters) and Outsiders (geeks, nerds, greasers, burnouts, band fags, etc.). Too often, the pack mentality of the team turned into exclusion or violence or rape.

The response to the column was overwhelming, thoughtful, and sometimes emotional, mostly from middle-aged men who remembered high school with pain and in some cases guilt that had darkened the rest of their lives.

Several years later, reading the obits of World Trade Center victims, I was struck by how many had defined themselves as athletes or fans. Personnel executives told me they specifically tried to hire former high school and college athletes for brokerage jobs because they had discipline, were responsive to authority, knew how to overcome setbacks, and were willing to play hurt—that is, come to work sick. The firefighters, police officers, and emergency technicians who rushed in exemplified Jock Culture's most heroic and selfless models. On the other hand, what was the president's preening "Mission Accomplished" turn but a macho parody of a Super Bowl-winning quarterback?

Jock Culture even reached into that most sacred of precincts, *The New York Times*. In 2001, right after he was named executive editor but before he occupied that perch, Howell Raines took the sports department to lunch. He contemptuously dismissed the previous administration and promised us a new era of hard-driving, zone-flooding creative tension in which he would run the paper the way Coach Bear Bryant ran the Alabama football team. Being sportswriters, we assumed this Coach Bullfrog was merely trying to out-jock us. Sportswriters are used to that, and like athletes we tend to offer sly servility to alpha males. We were wrong, of course. Raines was serious. It took the courage of the news nerds to drive him out of the arena.

* * *

At the end of 2002, Raines, who apparently never much liked my sports column, declined to renew my thirteenth consecutive annual contract. Less than six months later, after he was fired, the *Times* sent me a new contract. I never signed it. I had reentered my Gallico mode and was writing fiction full-time again, this time for good, I hoped.

But I couldn't stay away from Gallico's *Farewell*. What drew me back to it for the third read was the steroids story, particularly the anguished cries of the baseball wonks that Barry Bonds's chemically aided statistics had made a mockery of the game's history and should be erased or foot-noted. Who cares! I thought. (Unless you want to asterisk Babe Ruth's records: *Never batted against colored brothers.) What matters is the discrete joy of tonight's game, pitch by pitch, inning by inning. I remembered how touched I'd been at fifteen by Gallico's lyrical passages on baseball as theater, the beautiful geometry of it, the small dramas, the looming threat of a home run, the liberation from everyday life.

And so it was *Farewell* again, from the beginning.

This time I laughed out loud when Gallico described international figure skating as "joyously crooked" and the judges as "scamps and vote-peddlers." He knew this even before the French judge sold out to the Russians at the 2002 Winter Olympic Games. I was thrilled by his paean to cars at speed and to the auto racer as athlete. In the closest I'd come to Gallico's participatory journalism, I'd driven a stock car at 130 miles an hour while covering NASCAR in 2001. Drivers were certainly as athletic as "the stick-and-ballers." Gallico and I also agreed that horse racing was basically gambling, and that "college football today is one of the last great strongholds of genuine old-fashioned American hypocrisy." Gallico was railing about Yale selling its broadcast rights for $20,000.

One of the areas I reread with interest and trepidation was about women. I winced when Gallico wrote, "No matter how good they are, they can never be good enough, quite, to matter," but in a way he was right. How else explain why women's records, accomplishments, and attendance figures are always measured against men's? Why does Billie Jean King beating that old clown Bobby Riggs, or Michelle Wie, the Tigress Woods inching her way into the men's game, get so much more coverage than the revolution that Title IX has wrought in the everyday lives of girls and their families?

I think Gallico, if he were around, could have some fun in his column with the vulnerable veneer of our macho heroes—if it didn't interfere with booking them for his TV and radio shows. He'd have to deal with jock girls calling each other "fag" for intimidation or motivation. He'd also have to explain why male pro athletes are terrified of having open gays in their locker rooms lest their relatives, friends, and fans think they are gay too.

Gallico would have flourished in today's atmosphere, been a multi-platform star like Mike Lupica, Stephen A. Smith, Sally Jenkins, Frank Deford, Tony Kornheiser, Christine Brennan, Jason Whitlock, and John

Feinstein. Gallico would know the territory, be smart enough to navigate Jock Culture and snipe at it, be enough of a believer to never attack it systemically. While the new diversity of the current press box has sensitized coverage, the biggest problem remains the widening distance between reporter and subject—except where ex-jocks playing reporters on TV manage to straddle the gap. I have no doubt that Gallico would find a way to walk the line with style, confidence, and residuals.

I probably won't read *Farewell* again cover to cover, but the presence of Gallico's papers at Columbia University teases me. Maybe I should write about him since, after all, this piece was about me. But then I'd have to deal with Gallico's best piece of advice, the one I mentioned earlier: "Your circulation begins to fall off if you destroy too many illusions, especially if you yourself have created them."

Marla Cone

—

RACHEL CARSON'S
SILENT SPRING

As a crop duster swooped down over a row of vegetables in California's Imperial Valley, I sat in a pickup truck, the windows rolled up. It was the spring of 1997 and I was investigating a story about efforts by Native American tribes to outlaw aerial spraying of pesticides. I was also five months pregnant, and when I embarked on the trip I rationalized that if I happened to be exposed to a single, minuscule dose of a pesticide, it wasn't going to do any harm. But at that moment, alone in the darkness, parked on a dirt road next to the field, I was having second thoughts.

I knew that the fetus I was carrying was the most vulnerable life on Earth when it came to the dangers of pesticides and other toxic chemicals. Was this story worth the risk—any risk, no matter how small? As I watched the plane unleash a trail of diluted insecticide, I noticed a fly inside the cab buzzing against the windshield. I decided that if it suddenly fell silent, I would start the ignition and take off. As absurd as it seems now, watching that fly manage to survive calmed me. At the time I chalked it up to the irrational obsession of a pregnant woman, but I now realize that the fly was my totem, a symbol straight out of Rachel Carson's *Silent Spring*.

Oddly enough, when I began covering environmental problems in the mid-1980s, I thought that *Silent Spring* was an anachronism, important only as a reminder of people's profound ignorance about the environment during the post–World War II industrial age. I was starting kindergarten in September of 1962 when Carson published her epic warning about how man-made pesticides were poisoning the world. Oblivious to what Carson called the "elixirs of death," I grew up on the shoreline of Lake Michigan, in one of the nation's toxic hotspots, Waukegan, Illinois, and during the time when the "Dirty Dozen"—the ubiquitous DDT and other toxic chlorinated chemicals—were reaching record levels in all our urban environments, particularly around the Great Lakes. Yet by the time I was a teenager in the 1970s, the world's worst environmental problems had supposedly been brought under control. We had seen the Evil Empire, and it was that of our fathers and mothers. We were the offspring of the clueless World War II generation that sprayed DDT and poisoned the Great Lakes and fouled the air. We were finding the solution to pollution.

But I now realize that what Carson called the "chain of evil"—the buildup of chemicals in our environment—continues unbroken to this day. And even though the political firestorm Carson's book stirred up forty-three years ago burns with just as much intensity today, most of Carson's science remains sound and her warnings prescient. If we take a mental snapshot of what we know now about the dangers of chemical exposure, the questions still outnumber the answers. Yet one thing remains as certain as it was in 1962: we are leaving a toxic trail that will outlive us.

* * *

The first chapter of *Silent Spring*, "Fable for Tomorrow," is one of the grimmest scenes in American literature, fact or fiction. "There was once a town in the heart of America where all life seemed to live in harmony with its surroundings," Carson begins. It was a glorious place. Birds chirped, fish jumped, foxes barked, trees and flowers were ablaze with color. "Then a strange blight crept over the area and everything began to change," she continues. Robins, jays, and scores of other songbirds disappeared, livestock were sickened, trees and flowers withered, streams were lifeless, children dropped dead suddenly while playing. "No witchcraft, no enemy action had silenced the rebirth of new life in this stricken world," Carson explains. "The people had done it themselves."

No such town actually existed. "But it might easily have a thousand counterparts in America or elsewhere in the world," Carson writes. A nature writer and aquatic biologist with the U.S. Fish and Wildlife Service, Carson had already written two best-sellers before she spent four years researching *Silent Spring*. She described in great scientific detail the dangers of DDT and its sister chlorinated chemicals, and her writings transformed how people felt about pesticides. After World War II, synthetic compounds were being invented on a daily basis, especially after the wonders of combining carbon and chlorine molecules had been discovered. DDT was first synthesized in the 1800s, and it was used in great volumes as an insecticide beginning in the 1940s. Its power was thought to be extraordinary because, although it killed bugs, it wasn't acutely poisonous and seemed relatively benign to everything but bugs. Soon, though, it became clear that DDT was dangerous in a slow, insidious sort of way. In the 1950s and 1960s, it began spreading worldwide, building up in oceans, waterways, and soil. It didn't easily break down in the environment, remaining in the food chain for decades. It collected in fat and tissues, passing from one animal to another—from plankton to worm to fish to bird, from hay to cow to milk to human child.

Silent Spring explained all that, and it became a phenomenal bestseller. No other environmental book has had such a far-reaching impact. Carson was a scientist, a journalist, and a crusader, and her book scared the hell out of people. She portrayed the science of the day in such dense detail that much of the 368-page book is too unwieldy, even today, for most readers to comprehend. Yet her gift as a writer was her eloquent and shocking prose, in which she philosophized about the ramifications of the science. Her words hastened the dawn of the environmental movement in the late 1960s, and by the early 1970s, the United States and most of the developed world had banned DDT and many other chlorinated compounds.

Carson's fabled world of the future, of course, has not materialized. But what's remarkable now when I reread *Silent Spring* is that the reality Carson described remains our own. DDT, PCBs, and related compounds remain in the tissues of virtually every living thing. They continue to spread globally, from pole to pole, via the air and ocean currents. Even eagles' eggs on Alaska's remote Aleutian Islands contain high levels of DDT despite the fact that the pesticide has never been sprayed there.

* * *

When the manuscript of *Silent Spring* was serialized in *The New Yorker* in June 1962, Carson was demonized. Chemical companies, and even some of her fellow scientists, attacked her data and interpretations, lambasted her credentials, called her hysterical and one-sided, and pressured her publisher, Houghton Mifflin, to withdraw *Silent Spring*. Monsanto went so far as to publish a parody of *Silent Spring*, called *The Desolate Year*, in which famine, disease, and insects take over the world after pesticides have been banned.

Carson is still the target of countless critiques. "DDT killed bald eagles because of its persistence in the environment. *Silent Spring* is now killing African children because of its persistence in the public mind," Tina Rosenberg wrote last year in a piece about malaria in *The New York Times Magazine* called "What the World Needs Now Is DDT." It's true that *Silent Spring* failed to describe the benefits of pesticides in fighting malaria, which is spread by mosquitoes, and in protecting food crops from destructive pests. Perhaps Carson believed that everyone acknowledged the benefits while ignoring the risks. Her goal, after all, was action, not contemplation.

Nevertheless, accusing *Silent Spring* of killing children in Africa is disingenuous. Most malaria experts, including the Malaria Foundation International, aren't rallying behind DDT. They support its limited use only until cost-effective substitutes are in place, perhaps in a few years. DDT remains one of the few cheap, effective tools used in the war against malaria, which kills more than two million people a year, mostly children in Africa. But unlike in the 1950s and 1960s, when up to 400,000 tons a year were sprayed from trucks and airplanes, the current practice is to spray only the interior walls of houses at risk.

When Carson was writing, it was considered cutting-edge science to determine whether a chemical mutated cells or triggered tumors, which explains why *Silent Spring* emphasizes the cancer risk of chemical compounds, a claim that looks a bit outdated today. Carson also had a personal reason for her warnings about carcinogens. She was diagnosed with breast cancer while writing *Silent Spring*, and it killed her at the age of fifty-six, less than two years after her book was published. Today there is little evidence of a link between DDT in women's bodies and the rate of breast cancer. Nevertheless, the cancer link has not been dismissed. Scientists wonder if brief exposure to DDT and other chemicals in the womb, rather than the amounts accumulated over a lifetime, can trigger cancer later in life.

Unbeknownst to Carson, chemicals at low doses have even more insidious dangers, beyond cancer. Scientists now believe that many industrial compounds and pesticides, including DDT, assault the innermost workings of living things—skewing brain development, sex hormones, and immune cells.

* * *

Carson accused those who extolled the virtues of pesticides of dispensing "little tranquilizing pills of half truth" and "sugar coating" unpalatable facts. "The public must decide whether it wishes to continue on the present road," she insisted, "and it can do so only when in full possession of the facts."

As a journalist, I know that is where I come in. For Carson, suffering from cancer, *Silent Spring* was her own personal heart of darkness, an excruciating journey into her own mind and the "sinister" world of chemicals. For me, writing about chemicals provokes its own inner turmoil as I seek certainty in an age of ambiguity. How do we square the risks of a chemical with its benefits? The precautionary principle, codified by the European Union, prescribes preventive measures when science is uncertain. The American philosophy prefers after-the-fact fixes rather than precautionary steps that may be excessive.

I was once accused of writing with "too much of the gravity of Rachel Carson." I wonder whether that's a weakness or a strength. After all, newspapers today tend to simplify issues related to environmental health and publish pieces that tell readers essentially nothing. We shouldn't unjustifiably scare readers, but we shouldn't bore them either. Most environmental journalists writing about toxic chemicals do one or the other. Those who bore readers haven't done the homework to understand the risks of certain chemicals and consequently are incapable of explaining those risks in terms people can understand. Those who scare readers don't put the risks in perspective or fail to reveal which chemicals and which exposures matter the most. We don't have to write with the grim foreboding of *Silent Spring* or the intentional exaggeration of its "Fable for Tomorrow," or ignore the benefits of the chemicals we rely upon today. But we do need to master Carson's skill for explaining what is at stake.

Carson's readers reacted with outrage, but many people today seem to prefer to remain ignorant of the risks of the chemicals they are routinely exposed to. "It is human nature to shrug off what may seem to us a vague threat of future disaster," Carson asserted, and that, in part, explains why the American mind-set remains closer to "better living through chemistry" than "better safe than sorry." I behave like any American consumer. I have resorted to sprinkling diazinon on anthills and passing over organic foods because they cost too much. I'm aware that my new mattress contains flame retardants and my nail polish has phthalates, but I bought them anyway. I haven't tossed out my polycarbonate food containers, and recently when my dentist filled a cavity, I chose an amalgam that contains a trace of mercury because it is more durable than the mercury-free alternatives.

Still, after nineteen years on the beat, I certainly know that the fly buzzing at the windshield was not a valid way to assess the dangers of pesticide exposure. When it comes to low doses we encounter in our daily lives, there are no dead bodies, no smoking guns. Many scientists now say the effects on children's brains and reproductive and immune systems are subtle, virtually impossible to pin down. Sometimes I think back to family dinners at a popular fish restaurant at Waukegan Harbor, which was later declared a Superfund site because of tons of PCBs dumped there, and wonder, usually in the most abstract and impersonal of ways, what effects the contaminants of that era had on me and my generation. Use of chlorinated compounds like DDT and PCBs peaked in the 1960s and tainted all our foods, even our mothers' breast milk, and children whose mothers ate a lot of PCB-tainted fish from Lake Michigan have lower IQs and worse memories, according to ten years of research conducted in Michigan. I also wonder, as only a mother could, whether my son suffered some slight neurological damage from the pesticides and other chemicals I was exposed to. He's healthy, he's smart. But could some neurotoxin explain why his handwriting is so sloppy and he has trouble tying his shoes? Absurd, you say? These worries, though, are the inevitable spinoff of this new generation of environmental science. These private musings have driven my desire to understand and explain to readers the risks of toxic chemicals, particularly to pregnant women and their newborns.

Until a few years ago, I felt reassured that the worst was over, that *Silent Spring* was so successful in its crusade against the most pervasive and persistent compounds that the book was no longer relevant. But I know

now that other chemicals are simply taking their place. Compounds still widely used in household products, farms, and factories are building up in animal and human bodies at an extraordinary pace, and some seem to have effects similar to the PCBs, DDT, and others that were banned decades ago. We have simply exchanged one risk for another.

The question we face about toxic pollutants is no longer "Do we want to save the world?" but "How safe do we want to be?" In the twenty-first century, our "Fable for Tomorrow" is not some disaster we are trying to avert but a vague, incalculable, and potentially serious threat to our children's health. We must remind readers that most environmental health decisions aren't a question of good versus evil. They amount to a judgment call, a trade-off. "We stand now where two roads diverge," Carson wrote in the final chapter of *Silent Spring*. "The choice, after all, is ours to make."

Ben Yagoda

—

WALTER BERNSTEIN'S
KEEP YOUR HEAD DOWN

At 5:30 a.m. on February 24, 1941, a twenty-one-year-old Dartmouth graduate named Walter Bernstein reported to Draft Board 179 in his native borough of Brooklyn. He and his fellow future soldiers were greeted by a member of the draft board: "a small, round, baldheaded man," Bernstein wrote later, "who came in smiling and rubbing his hands, and immediately knocked on a table for silence."

After calling out a roster, the man led the inductees outside.

They walked down the dark street toward the subway. The street lamps shone yellowly on the sad, dirty remains of the last snowfall. "I should have brought my rubbers," someone said. At the subway the baldheaded man stopped and took a pack of government transit tickets from his pocket. He gave these to the lead man, together with a printed list of instructions as to where he should go. Then he beamed at all the men and said in a loud voice, "Good luck, fellows." He waved cheerily as the men trooped down the subway stairs. "You little baldheaded son of a bitch," one of the men said, but the little man did not seem to hear.

Those words appeared in Bernstein's 1945 book, *Keep Your Head Down*. They provide a flavor of what makes the book so extraordinary. In clear-eyed, crisp, unsentimental, highly cinematic, and resolutely unjingoistic prose, Bernstein offered a sense of what it was like to experience World War II, from induction to discharge. The correspondents who got the most acclaim at the time, and who are read in the survey courses today, tended to be the Bigfeet: Liebling with the big voice, Hemingway with the big irony, Hersey with the big story, Ernie Pyle with the big heart. Bernstein was a miniaturist by nature, and as such was and is easy to look past. His work bears a resemblance to Pyle's, but the differences are telling. Pyle had been a newspaperman for two decades when he started covering the war, and in his pieces you feel that he had taken on the official role of Chronicler of the American GI: he was polished, occasionally sentimental, always sympathetic, and inevitably a bit at arm's length from the men he was writing about. Bernstein was an enlisted man; the view from the ground was the view he saw. It is a view that today's embedded reporters, despite a wealth of gadgetry that brings Iraq into our living rooms, are unable to deliver. Bernstein's grunt's-eye perspective, combined with his literary talent and his innate skepticism, produced meticulously observed set pieces that evoked the near-constant fear, uncertainty, and hunger felt by men involved in achieving profoundly unspectacular objectives—the fog of war, as the currently popular formulation goes. As he wrote in one of the chapters, ironically titled "I Love Mountain Warfare" (about playing cat-and-mouse with the Germans in the Italian mountains):

> The night was like all other nights. We stumbled down one mountain and crawled up another. We crossed a stream with the water up to our knees. No one talked; no one sang. We didn't know where we were going or what we would find when we got there. Some of the officers might have known, but they probably weren't very sure. We didn't know where the enemy was. We didn't even know where we were. We just walked. There was nothing at all nice about the walk. It was dirty, tiring, dangerous and without immediate compensation, and it was exactly what this war was like to most of the men in it. No matter how they felt about the war, this was how it was fought. And there were no Purple Hearts for either trench foot or jaundice.

Bernstein was something of a literary prodigy. By the time he reported to the draft board he'd already published short stories and sketches in *The New Yorker* and was working as a Broadway rewrite man. (His dream since childhood was to be a dramatist, which sheds light on all the dialogue and stage directions and economical characterization in his journalism.) After being sent to Fort Benning, Georgia, for basic training, he periodically mailed off to the magazine accounts of his experiences. The pieces that were published showed a nice ear and eye for the banter and bravado and busywork camouflaging the pervasive jitters of the pre–Pearl Harbor period. In "Action in Georgia," parts of which read like a treatment for Abbott and Costello's movie *Buck Privates*, Bernstein describes the men, including Stein, "a twenty-five-year-old Brooklyn clothing salesman," ribbing their sergeant in double-talk:

> Stein had his rifle over his knee and was gesturing toward the inner parts. "The kravaswitch is broken," he was saying.
> "You mean the bolt?" the sergeant asked.
> "He means the kravasnatch," another man said. "The part next to the warple."
> The sergeant picked up the rifle and inspected it carefully.
> "It's broken," Stein said firmly. "The lieutenant said I should show it to you."
> "Looks OK to me," the sergeant said. He stared doubtfully at the rifle and then at the men, but no one laughed. "Beats me," he said finally. He handed the rifle back to Stein, and then everyone laughed.
> "What a connivo," one of the men said, hitting Stein on the back.
> The sergeant didn't look too pleased but he smiled. "I thought it was some of your Jew talk," he said to Stein.

While at Fort Benning, Bernstein was assigned to write the book for a musical comedy meant to entertain the troops. This was so successful that he was transferred to New York to work on a similar but much larger-scale effort, Irving Berlin's Broadway revue *This Is the Army*. Bernstein duly put together his behind-the-scenes observations in an article meant for *The New Yorker*. Then came trouble. A colonel got hold of the manuscript, decided that it ridiculed the army, and decreed that if it saw print, Bernstein would be punished, perhaps by court martial.

Bernstein reported this turn of events to Harold Ross, *The New Yorker's* editor. As Bernstein (who is, as the saying goes, very much alive) recounted in his 1996 memoir, *Inside Out*, Ross

> was delighted. As a private in World War One he had edited the army newspaper, *Stars and Stripes*, and relished any fight with the brass. . . . While I waited in his office, Ross got on the phone to General George Marshall, the army chief of staff in Washington. Marshall had been an aide to General John J. Pershing, who commanded the American Expeditionary Force in the First War, and Ross had known him then. What I could hear of the conversation was jovially profane. When he hung up, Ross turned to me with a big, gap-toothed smile and announced it was all taken care of.

Not only would the article run, but Bernstein was assigned to be a reporter for *Yank*, a new weekly magazine staffed entirely by enlisted men. Bernstein spent a few months in New York, where *Yank* had its offices, then sailed across the Atlantic Ocean on a Dutch freighter. He put in some time in Tehran, Cairo, and Tel Aviv (where he played touch football on the beach with Irwin Shaw), but there were few stories and no combat. So he hitched a ride on an attack bomber heading to Sicily.

* * *

Bernstein's situation, once he got to the shooting war, was singular even by 1942 standards; today, it sounds like a fantasy. "I would get out on the road with my bedroll and typewriter and pistol and wander until I found a unit that promised a story," he recalled in *Inside Out*. Odder still, he wrote whatever he chose. Like the current-day journalists in the Persian Gulf, he was embedded, with the important difference that he was himself a soldier and would participate in any mission his unit was involved in.

Bernstein filed short reports for *Yank* but saved the good stuff for *The New Yorker*. Here, again, he was working without a net: he came up with his ideas and composed his stories on his own, then sent them to William Shawn (Ross's deputy and eventual successor), who usually accepted them. These pieces are the heart of *Keep Your Head Down*, out of which they pop with absolute freshness.

The best piece in the book—one of the best short works of wartime journalism ever—is "Search for a Battle." Bernstein is now on the mainland of Italy, though in his literary treatment the landscape has an existential anonymity. He is supposed to be woken up at two o'clock one morning to join a battalion attacking "a long steep ridge that stood like a door at the head of the valley we occupied," but in a typical foul-up, the message to rouse him gets lost. Setting off by himself to try to find the battalion, he hitches a ride across a field that's supposed to be mined, presses on by foot, and encounters the wounded, the desperate, and two burned-out infantrymen—black-comic characters out of *Waiting for Godot*:

> "We just got relieved," the rifleman said. "Only nobody knows where we're supposed to go."
> "I ain't even sure we been relieved," the mortar man said.
> "I'm sure," the rifleman said. "The lieutenant come by and said we were relieved. That's good enough for me."
> "The lieutenant got killed," the other man said.
> "So what?" the rifleman said. "He relieved us before he got killed."

Still separated from the battalion, Bernstein finds himself in a valley under shell attack and is unknowingly in the crosshairs of an enemy tank until some GIs summon him into their homemade shelter. He thanks them for saving his life; one of them replies, "Hell, he might have missed you."

The last chapter of the book is a long account of Bernstein's one authentic scoop. In Cairo, he befriended some Yugoslav partisans and arranged through them to go on a weeklong foot journey to the Yugoslav town of Drvar, where Bernstein had an exclusive interview with the partisan leader, Tito. After the story came out in *Yank*, *The New York Times* ran a front-page story about it.

Keep Your Head Down was well received. *The New York Times Book Review* remarked that "the stories of combat . . . have the ring of genuine authenticity." There was an Armed Services edition, and a Book Find Club reprint sold 40,000 copies. The book fell out of print soon after that, which in retrospect is not surprising. Postwar America was not especially in the mood for a rueful reminder of what it felt like to be cold and hungry and lost and trudging through the mud. That perspective, of course, is part of why the book doesn't feel dated by a day. It also offers a very clean first draft of an important slice of history.

After being discharged by the army, Bernstein became a staff reporter at *The New Yorker*, a loosely designed job for which he was not well suited.

He spent his afternoons going to the movies, in part because, as he wrote in *Inside Out*, "the alternative was sitting in my office and staring at a blank piece of paper." But there were other reasons. Even as a journalist he was a sort of scriptwriter, making certain, as he says now, that "every piece I wrote had some kind of set piece in it"; animating plays and players turned out to be his calling. The success of *Keep Your Head Down* earned him a movie contract. He spent six months in Hollywood, working on screenplays that included *All the King's Men* and *Kiss the Blood off My Hands*, then returned to New York to find that live television dramas were all the rage and that they needed scripts!

Bernstein tells the story of what happened next in *Inside Out*, and also in his 1976 screenplay for *The Front*. He was a Communist—not a sympathizer or fellow traveler, but a card-carrying meeting attender. Inevitably, he was blacklisted. Like the Woody Allen character in the movie, he survived by finding friendly civilians, or "fronts," who would sign their names to his scripts. Bernstein was unblacklisted in 1960, when United Artists hired him to work on the screenplay for *The Magnificent Seven*. Since then he has been busy and productive, with such credits as *Fail-Safe, Semi-Tough, Yanks, The House on Carroll Street*, and the 1997 HBO film *Miss Evers' Boys*, for which he won an Emmy.

***

As I write, there is a war going on, and among its many differences from World War II is the nature of the prose it has generated. Walter Bernstein was one of thousands of current and future writers drafted into service. He produced outstanding journalism; his counterparts refracted their experience into fiction (Norman Mailer, Irwin Shaw, James Jones, Joseph Heller, Kurt Vonnegut), poetry (Karl Shapiro, Randall Jarrell), drama, film, and even humor. Those talented chroniclers saw to it that the war was in an important sense a shared national experience.

With some notable exceptions (like Anthony Swofford and Joel Turnipseed, authors respectively of *Jarhead* and *Baghdad Express*), the all-volunteer army doesn't attract many literary types. We have the brave and sometimes eloquent embedded reporters, but they're mainly producing stories about "the organization"—strategy and training, objectives and preparedness, mission and manpower. Even when they attempt to turn from macro to micro, they are inevitably, like Ernie Pyle, at arm's length from the grunt on the ground—able to share his tent but not the feeling in his gut.

The result is an unfortunate irony. As we often hear, digital communication has made the world a smaller place. We can see the troops in Iraq in real time. Yet their experience remains profoundly remote and distant from us at home. A book like *Keep Your Head Down* reminds us of a time when a talented writer, utilizing a manual typewriter and airmail, could make his home-front readers feel what making war was like.

Evan Cornog

A. J. LIEBLING'S
THE EARL OF LOUISIANA

Southern political personalities, like sweet corn, travel badly. They
lose flavor with every hundred yards away from the patch. By the
time they reach New York, they are like Golden Bantam that has
been trucked up from Texas—stale and unprofitable. The consumer
forgets that the corn tastes different where it grows. That, I suppose, is why for twenty-five years I underrated Huey Pierce Long.

Thus begins A. J. Liebling's profile of Huey Long's brother, Earl, which
ran in *The New Yorker* in 1960 and was published as a book the following year. The lead demonstrates authorial self-confidence at the highest
level—here is a master, secure that whither he goes, his reader will follow.
It also establishes an important point—things are more complicated with
the Longs than they first appear to be (and that's pretty complicated).

At the book's start, Earl Long is the sitting governor of Louisiana
and is planning to run for reelection, in spite of a provision of the state
constitution barring a governor from succeeding himself. Earl's idea was
simple: he would win the Democratic primary, at that time tantamount
to election, and then resign. That way he would be succeeding not himself
but his short-term successor. As Liebling observes, "Even Huey had not
thought of that one." Earl's goal was a remarkable one not only in view
of the constitutional obstacle but also because a few months before Li-

ebling started reporting, the governor had "gone off his rocker" and been committed by his wife and family to a mental hospital in Texas. Long had managed to engineer his release, return to Louisiana, and resume his office, and then "he had departed on a long tour of recuperation at out-of-state Western racetracks."

In the rich and diverse cultures of Louisiana, Liebling found a setting perfect for his talents, and in Earl Long he found a character profoundly sympathetic. Liebling likes his characters fat and sassy, and Earl's oversized personality and intemperate appetites struck a chord in his biographer. Liebling affectionately records the governor's appearing with other politicians on the campaign trail, trading wisecracks with the crowd, cooling himself in the hot Louisiana evening with a handkerchief dipped in iced Coca-Cola, and "monopolizing attention like an old vaudeville star cast in a play with a gang of Method actors." Yet the political situation Liebling found in the state, which at first seemed the stuff of broad comedy, turned out to have the makings of a modern tragedy. The result, published as *The Earl of Louisiana*, is a masterwork of nonfiction writing.

Liebling generates fresh ideas, elegant turns of phrase, startling but apposite references, and sheer linguistic pleasure at a rate matched by no other journalist. An oilman is described as having "the kind of head Norman peasants carve on wooden stoppers for Calvados bottles." He mentions how, following President Eisenhower's heart attack, statements by physicians had become as newsworthy "as the award of an honorary degree to the publisher of the paper." Nearly every page holds something one wishes to read aloud to a friend.

It is also, in the wake of Hurricane Katrina, a tremendously moving tribute to the city of New Orleans, which Liebling discovers to lie outside the normal cultural boundaries of the United States, existing "within the orbit of the Hellenistic world that never touched the North Atlantic." Here's his description of this process of cultural migration: "The Mediterraneans who settled the shores of the interrupted sea scurried across the gap between the Azores and Puerto Rico like a woman crossing a drafty hall in a sheer nightgown to get to a warm bed with a man in it."

Liebling is an omnipresent narrator, and reading *The Earl of Louisiana* is like having a superb meal with the most entertaining of dinner partners. Characters are delineated with vivid economy. A leader in the local Democratic organization is depicted "squatting on a kitchen chair, like a great, wise, sun-freckled toad." Earl's late brother Huey is introduced this way:

"A chubby man, he had ginger hair and tight skin that was the color of a sunburn coming on. It was an uneasy color combination, like an orange tie on a pink shirt." In Earl Long's speeches, the governor's thoughts "chased one another on and off the stage like characters in a Shakespearean battle scene, full of alarums and sorties."

There are digressions aplenty in the book, but they just make for a more enjoyable experience, especially since Liebling's asides have a way of turning out to be more than pleasant detours. A host of seemingly tangential subjects—boxing, food, horseracing, resemblances between Louisiana politics and factional struggles in Lebanon—appear first as asides, then grow into themes, knitting together a sometimes unruly narrative, one in which the protagonist, the governor, does not appear in person until a third of the way into the book. The *opera buffa* story of Earl Long, which is where the story starts, begins to fade as the hero's progress is impeded (Long is prevented from pursuing his electoral scheme by the Democratic state committee), and then a more sinister story line takes over when the race for governor develops into a full-fledged white-supremacy campaign.

* * *

The opening sections of the book give little hint of the more serious issues that lie ahead. Liebling embraces both the grit and the shine of New Orleans, singing the praises of its food (in particular of "busters"—"fat softshell crabs shorn of their limbs, which are to the buster-fancier as trifling as a mustache on the plat du jour must seem to a cannibal").

The city of New Orleans, in fact, emerges as one of the leading characters, and its gin mills and strip clubs are rendered with affectionate care. The election, however, is for governor of the entire state, and north of the city the Catholic, Mediterranean flavor gives over to the more familiar Anglophone, Protestant South of northern Louisiana, where Liebling and a companion decide to head, having been in the Big Easy for so long, he explains, "we were beginning to pick up rumors that we ourselves had started."

It is a transition that Liebling conveys through a culinary observation. Stopping for a meal beyond the civilizing reach of New Orleans, they encounter a fry shack with "the shrimps stiff with inedible batter, the coffee desperate." Not yet a day out of New Orleans, Liebling is pining. "A PoBoy at Mumfrey's in New Orleans is a portable banquet," he rhapsodizes. "In the South proper, it is a crippling blow to the intestine."

This culinary shift as one travels north is symptomatic of a larger change, and Liebling describes the middle of Louisiana as the place "where the culture of one great thalassic littoral impinges on the other." It was the achievement of the Longs, both Huey and Earl, to recast the state's politics, winning the votes of poor voters of varied backgrounds and from all over the state, rather than choosing one side or the other of the thalassic divide. And, by the Southern standards of the time, Earl Long seemed to Liebling so temperate on racial matters that he describes him as "the only effective Civil Rights man in the South." The style of civil rights the Longs espoused, however, was hardly a paradise for African Americans. One example given is Huey Long's approach to getting jobs in state hospitals for African American nurses—he pretended to be outraged to discover that white nurses were taking care of black patients, saying such work was an affront to white womanhood. "It was the most racist talk you ever heard," an informant tells Liebling, "but the result was he got the white nurses out and the colored nurses in."

At times, the treatment of the race issue in the book seems strained and anachronistic, like the use of "colored" in the previous sentence. After all, Earl Long could be described as "the only effective Civil Rights man in the South" only by someone whose frame of reference was limited to white politicians. And there are scenes that can put today's reader on edge. At about the midpoint of the book, Liebling describes a dinner at the governor's mansion with Earl and a group of cronies. During the dinner a black waitress named Laura is called upon to perform an imitation of her prizefighter husband, which she does at some length.

"'Show us how your husband does when he gets tagged,' the Governor ordered, and Laura fell forward, her arms hanging over the invisible ropes, her head outside the ring, her eyes bulged and senseless.

"The feudal faces were red with mirth. I applauded as hard as I could. Laura stood up and curtsied." Liebling's complicity in this scene is tempered by his frank recognition, in the use of the word "feudal," of its true character. His depiction pays tribute both to the skill of Laura's enactment of her minstrel-show part and to the larger context in which it must be understood. Four decades later, we may not like watching it, but we can't deny that the scene is revealing.

This same sort of prestidigitation is achieved in the book's treatment of its larger subject, the political use of race and racial fear in Louisiana politics at the dawn of the 1960s. Once Earl was sidelined from the gubernatorial race, the principal contenders for the Democratic nomination were DeLesseps S. "Chep" Morrison, the New Orleans mayor; Jimmie Davis, a singer and former governor of the state who had had a big hit years earlier with "You Are My Sunshine, My Only Sunshine"; and Willie Rainach, the most outspoken segregationist in the state legislature. There were also two Longites running, and Earl was on the ballot for lieutenant governor. In the first round of the primary, Morrison came in first and Davis second, and these two faced each other in the runoff. But third place had gone to Rainach, and the support of his backers was seen as the key to victory. Morrison won the bulk of the black vote in the first round, and that left him open to charges from the racists that he was "soft" on segregation. So Davis (who had avoided the race issue in the first primary) quickly recast himself as a champion of segregation to line up support from Rainach. Eventually Earl Long himself announced he would vote for Davis (having apparently decided that having some influence with the likely winner was better than trying to make peace with a man he had offended by calling "Dellasoups").

The runoff election was a nasty, race-baiting affair, and Liebling describes it with unconcealed contempt. He recounts such "issues" as the accusation that Davis had once danced with Lena Horne at an event in California (as the Rainach forces, "the extreme faction of the bug-eyed," charged in the first primary), or the charge that Morrison had made an integrationist remark at the dedication of a swimming pool for blacks in 1948 (he hadn't). The climax of Liebling's exploration of the mind-set of racism is an interview with a New Orleans surgeon who confidently explains how the Fourteenth Amendment was the "bastard child" of Thaddeus Stevens and his "mulatto mistress." At the outset of the interview, he describes a couple of the surgeon's remarks as *amuse-gueules*, but as their conversation proceeds Liebling fades into the background. Knowing when to keep still, Liebling allows this "bleached in the bone" racist to expose his own vileness unmolested.

* * *

Today, of course, Liebling is best remembered as a press critic, and throughout the book he remains attentive to the misdeeds of the press, and in particular to those of the New Orleans *Times-Picayune*, which opposed the Longs. Liebling notes how newspaper photos of Earl "were usually taken without warning while he was scratching his pants, or when a reporter acting as the photographer's picador had provoked him into a scream of rage." He accuses *The Times-Picayune* of being willing to bring race relations in Louisiana down to the level of Mississippi "so long as *The Times-Picayune* could say it had elected a governor." (While many of the problems Liebling found in Louisiana persist, *The Times-Picayune* is a different newspaper today.)

On election night, Liebling moves around New Orleans following the returns, and it is at a bar run by an old prizefighter that he learns that Davis has finally overcome Morrison's initial lead from the early reporting New Orleans precincts and is moving toward victory based on his strength in the northern part of the state. Liebling's disgust grows deeper when Davis, once in office, moves to reward his racist supporters by backing a measure to throw illegitimate children off the welfare rolls in the state, a move that threatens those children with starvation. (British citizens sent donations to ease the suffering.) Liebling's account notes that the "net saving to the state of Louisiana" from this move would be $1.3 million, "a handsome return for starving 22,000 children to death." His final sentence is a postscript noting that the racists have "taken over the streets of New Orleans," with the state government cheering them on.

Liebling has marched a long way from his opening, with its cheery likening of Southern politicians to sweet corn. In Earl Long, the author found a kindred spirit—stout, fond of food and horseracing, quotably frank, and unwilling to adapt to the pieties of Ike's America. But Liebling was too good a reporter to miss the tragedy that lurked behind the farce that first drew him to Louisiana, and he takes the reader down that road of discovery at a time when coverage of the racial disparities of the South, and of the nation, was still highly intermittent in the mainstream American press.

Today, with the Hellenistic city that Liebling loved deeply wounded, the book seems like a chunk of literary amber, preserving lost New Orleans for future generations, as Lawrence Durrell preserved Egyptian Alexandria and James Joyce preserved his Dublin. Hold it up to the light, and see what it reveals.

Ted Conover

—

STANLEY BOOTH'S
THE TRUE ADVENTURES OF
THE ROLLING STONES

In 1984, when I was beginning my book *Coyotes*, my editor at Random House handed me a brand new book about the Rolling Stones that he said was very, very good. The editor, David Rosenthal, had just come to the book business from *Rolling Stone* magazine and so, I figured, knew what he was talking about. I browsed *Dance with the Devil: The Rolling Stones and Their Times*, by Stanley Booth, noticing that much of it took place in 1969, during a tour of the United States that ended with the infamous Altamont concert in California. "Why's it only coming out now?" I asked Rosenthal, who grimaced. "Long story," he said, and never told it to me.

I do not read many books about music, but this one drew me in. Part of the reason was that Booth's style of research with the famous rock group seemed similar to what I had in mind with Mexican migrants: participate and immerse rather than simply interview and observe. Yes, the Rolling Stones on tour led a life different in most respects from that of people sneaking into the United States, but there were similarities (young men traveling in a group, young men working but also having an adventure, young men breaking laws, young men staying up late and getting blasted, etc.). The other reason was that, as I soon discovered, *Dance with the Devil* is a treasure of participatory journalism, a book with something good on practically every page.

It was also a book suited to the disjointed way in which I was living at the time. *Dance with the Devil*, in other words, though mainly about a tour, digresses frequently and does not impel you breathlessly toward the end. So I could read it in little pieces, a few pages here and a few pages there; unlike most books that I don't plunge into, it remained at hand. Maybe because those early days were also a time when I often found myself stuck in writing, too self-critical and unable to find the words, Booth's book also came to hold a sort of magic for me, the power to break a dam and start a flow. Which is more, somehow, than I can say for most books I admire.

The hardcover edition didn't sell and so the paperback was retitled (in the way the author had always wanted): *The True Adventures of the Rolling Stones*. But that didn't help sales either and both editions soon fell out of print. In 2000, however, *True Adventures* got a new life when it was republished by Chicago's A Cappella Press. Blurbs on the cover, I was delighted to see, showed that it had found other admirers. "The one authentic masterpiece of rock 'n' roll writing," raved Peter Guralnick, a writer not given to hyperbole (or blurbs, for that matter). There was a new afterword too, so I picked up a copy and read the book again.

True Adventures begins in a way that gives readers a taste of what they're in for, and foreshadows the disaster to come. Six strange paragraphs in italics, a kind of prologue, describe Mick and Keith's nighttime reconnoiter of the coming evening's venue, the Altamont Speedway east of San Francisco, where they would give a long-awaited free concert:

> *It is late. All the little snakes are asleep. The world is black outside the car windows, just the dusty clay road in the headlights. Far from the city, past the last crossroads (where they used to bury suicides in England, with wooden stakes driven through their hearts), we are looking for a strange California hillside where we may see him, may even dance with him in his torn, bloody skins, come and play.*

Inside the band's limo, The Crystals are on the radio singing "He's a Rebel." Outside, people waiting for the gates to open are everywhere, with their dogs, packs, and sleeping bags. The driver doesn't know where to go but finally arrives at a fence. "So we stand on one foot and then the other, swearing in the cold, and no one comes to let us in, and the gate, which is leaning, rattles when I shake it, and I say we could push it down pretty easy, and Keith says, 'The first act of violence.'"

The story of the free concert, which is well known, ends the book: as the Stones play the next night, the Hell's Angels, acting as security, will kill a black man and beat others. Altamont is considered by many to be the calamity that began the eclipse of the Age of Aquarius. Ending the italicized section is a cartoon panel with the title, "J. P. Alley: Hambone's Meditations." The black man pictured in it, leading a mule, is saying, "O, lock up de do' en set down yo' load—hones' folks asleep en de debil on de road!!"

It's the only drawing in the book and, with its racist dialect, its presence seemed strange—until I discovered that "Hambone's Meditations" was until 1968 a regular feature of the Memphis *Commercial Appeal*. Then I saw how it ties together three important elements of Booth's project: Memphis, where he began his career writing about the blues (he is originally from Georgia), the Stones's satanism, and black people (and their music and their rhymes) as depicted by white people. Because what apparently drew Booth to the Stones was music: they were set apart from most other acts by their interest in and adoption of the blues, and Booth's association with that music, and the South, seems to have been a reason they agreed to let him chronicle their tour.

That chronicling gets under way after passages about the formation of the Stones, their rise to popularity in Britain, and the death of the guitarist Brian Jones, apparently from a drug overdose. Booth also re-creates early meetings with the Stones and their managers, repeatedly sharing his anxiety over whether the arrangement will work out, whether he'll have a deal signed before the tour begins. As Booth tells it, what probably clinches the deal is when Jagger asks him:

"What would your book be about?"
"About?"
"You know, what would be in it?"
"What will be in your next song?"
"A girl in a barroom, man, I don't know. It's much easier to write a song than a book," says Jagger. . . .
I told Mick that I had written a story about a blues singer who had swept the streets in Memphis for more than forty years, but he's more than just a street sweeper, because he's never stopped playing, if you see what I mean. I didn't look at Mick to find out whether he saw. You write, I told him, about things that move your

heart, and in the story about the old blues singer I wrote about where he lives and the songs he sings and just lists of the things he swept up in the streets, and I can't explain to him, Furry Lewis, what it is about him that moves my heart, and I can't tell you what I would write about the Rolling Stones, and so, well, I guess I can't answer your question. No, he said, you answered it, and for the first time since I thought, long months ago, of writing this book, I felt almost good about it.

It's when the tour begins, in the book's middle section, that the ship leaves the shore and Booth finds his pace. He is with the band during rehearsals, at arena gigs, and inside recording sessions, cars, private jets, hotel suites, and house parties with a changing cast of groupies, handlers, cops, and other musicians. Booth has said in an interview that "I wanted to write a book that readers could walk around in and know what it was like to be in London in 1968 or America in 1969," and he works hard to capture the texture of the times.

He is strongest when writing about the music—the history of it, the business of it, and the experience of it. Booth's believer's passion results in all sorts of luminous insights into the enterprise: "The Stones's show was not a concert but a ritual; their songs . . . were acts of violence, brief and incandescent." And later, "Making love and death into songs was exactly the Stones's business." Booth tells a story in which "each night we went someplace new and strange and yet similar to the place before, to hear the same men play the same songs to kids who all looked the same, and yet each night it was different, each night told us more." He suggests that "in the sixties we believed in a myth—that music had the power to change people's lives. Today people believe in a myth—that music is just entertainment." He writes about what it was like backstage and what it was like in the audience, what it felt like when things really clicked and what it was like when they did not.

The backstage view is, of course, the main draw to a book like this, and Booth offers anecdotes intriguing, disgusting, and amusing. He writes about a comely woman in the studio audience during the taping of *The Ed Sullivan Show* who does not succeed in getting taken advantage of: a minion picks a "big blond in buckskin" to visit the boys backstage instead. Booth writes of leaving the studio with a friend, "the pretty little girl in

the brown outfit ahead of us, smiling, lucky to be left with her dreams."
He reports on how, a couple of days after a recording session, the Stones
"made more money than they had ever made in one day by recording a
television commercial for Rice Krispies. . . ." In one particularly delightful
scene, Booth describes Jagger on his hotel bed after a concert, exhausted,
eating Chinese food, and taking flack from others for his smelly socks:

> Mick drew his feet up under him . . . and began talking to me about
> the future, where to live, what to do. . . . "I've got to find a place to
> live, got to think about the future, because obviously I can't do *this*
> forever." He rolled his eyes. "I mean, we're so old—we've been go-
> ing on for eight years and we can't go on for another eight. I mean,
> if you can you will do, but I just can't, I mean we're so old—Bill's
> *thirty-three.*"

Sometimes there's just pleasure in the writerly risks Booth takes, and
seeing how they pay off. Toward the end of the tour, he describes wak-
ing up at the Plaza Hotel in New York "still anesthetized by the heroin."
His friend, Gore, "being like all speed freaks evangelistic," takes him to a
"speed doctor," who gives them shots in the butt of something restorative
for ten dollars apiece. Booth then writes:

> I had felt faint and limp-wristed, but with the charge in my ass I
> decided we didn't need a cab, we could walk across town to Madi-
> son Square Garden for the Stones's afternoon concert. Out of an
> earnest desire not to rob this account of its true interest, I will
> confess that I was carrying the red carnation from my bedside table
> at the Plaza; so there I went, boots, jeans, and leather jacket, sniff-
> ing a long-stemmed red carnation, looking like some insane faggot
> ought to be kilt with a shovel, as we walked briskly through the
> streets, fatigue gone, feeling ardent.

* * *

What Booth captures so well is the particular energy of the time. The style
is sometimes Beat, Kerouacian—there's a sense of experimentation under
way. And in that, *True Adventures* achieves true oneness with its subject:
like the Stones, Booth is full of aspiration, trying something new, unsure
where it will take him. And that, in retrospect, is I think the book's great

resonance for me, and its promise for any young writer: take these chances, it has continued to tell me, and some of them will pay off.

The Random House cover photo of the author, apparently taken years later, showing him neatly groomed and wearing coat and tie, made you wonder how on earth he hung out with the Stones. But a much better shot of Booth and Keith Richards at the end of the new edition shows him long-haired and modish, bandanna around his neck, perhaps backstage somewhere, looking like maybe Keith's brother. (Throughout *True Adventures* he seems to connect more readily with Keith, and, indeed, years later he published another book about only him: *Keith: Standing in the Shadows*.)

This photo is a valuable addition because it lets you see how close Booth got to the band, how much he identified with them. And by contrast, how little common ground he felt with other journalists on the Stones' trail. Take, for instance, Booth's descriptions of the Stones' press conferences and interviews with the correspondents of various well-known media. The distance between these accomplished people and the author is fascinating. Instead of participating in these scenes, he simply observes cannily, letting the reporters' superficial questions and the Stones' sound-bite answers speak for themselves. It's all summed up by a sentence which, when he wrote it, must have given Booth great pleasure: "When the *Newsweek* talk ended and the reporter left, we all decided to have lunch together on the Strip."

At other times, his in-group status results in clear antipathy toward outsiders. He's particularly hard on Albert and David Maysles, who are also along for parts of the tour, including Altamont, filming their now-classic documentary, *Gimme Shelter*. The filmmakers' sin, it appears, is to have gained access to the inner sanctum without the requisite knowledge of the music, or long-term commitment to the enterprise. Booth is in a New York taxi with the brothers on the last day of the tour: "As we rode we talked about the Stones. David and Al seemed to know nothing about them and two months later, after their film was shot, would still be talking about Bill Watts" (a conflation of the names of Charlie Watts, the drummer, and Bill Wyman, the bass player).

* * *

Another peril of participatory journalism is exposure to a subject's vices—drugs, in the case of the Rolling Stones. Drug use was part of the ethic of the times. "Practically everybody who got near the band in those days got drug-addicted," a friend whose family was in business with them told me. Booth comments on it (and has joked that the book was so late because he had to wait for statutes of limitation to expire). And yet Booth also, in being so firmly "embedded" with the Stones, seems unaware of what he's being swallowed up by—or, at any rate, unwilling to struggle against it. Booth, with Richards apparently as his source, maintains that in the early days the Stones took "no dope of any kind. . . . But in 1969 things had changed. It would be impossible to endure a world that makes you work and suffer, impossible to endure history, if it weren't for the fleeting moments of ecstasy." And so we have the drugs, and the justification for them. By the seventh paragraph of the tour, Booth is taking up a roadie for B. B. King on his offer of a sniff of heroin and then describing how particularly sexy Tina Turner and the Ikettes looked when he was high, how it figured in with the work ("People talked to me but I went on writing, no one could reach me in my Poe-like drugged creative sweats"). Marijuana is omnipresent, starting on page four. In one passage, Booth, tripping on LSD, describes a policeman in a roadside café, "all dark blue, black leather, and menacing devices." The cop, on his radio, receives a report of a crime committed by a black teenage girl. "The cop said he'd be right there, his tone loaded with sex and sadism. The only way he could be intimate with a black girl was to punish her. After he left, the place still reeked with his lust, if you had taken acid."

After all these years, I finally see that drug use probably explains the book's hallucinatory opening (where else do you get, "All the little snakes are asleep" and the suicides with stakes through their hearts?), and I can see it behind some of the book's luminosity and its inscrutability. Booth makes clear that drug addiction was, indeed, one of the reasons the book took so long to complete; withdrawal, he writes, brought on epileptic seizures. But it apparently wasn't the main one. In the new afterword he lays the blame mainly on changing times, on the end of the sixties, on the rise of Reagan and yuppies and greed. He claims:

> I had to become a different person from the narrator in order to tell the story. This was necessary because of the heartbreak, the disappointment, the chagrin, the regret, the remorse. We had all, Stones, fans, hangers-on, parasites, observers, been filled with optimism

there in the autumn of 1969 . . . we believed that we were different, that we were somehow chosen, or anointed, for success, for love and happiness. We were wrong.

Elsewhere in the afterword, he writes that he had to overcome depression and "domestic upheaval." "So torn was I that at times I begged for death and for years tempted death almost constantly, at last throwing myself off a North Georgia mountain waterfall onto the granite boulders below, smashing my face, breaking my back."

What to make of this? Cynically, I now wonder if such a talented writer simply requires a dramatic explanation—for himself, as much as anyone—for his book being nearly fifteen years late. But a better part of me appreciates that journalism approaching this level of art might necessarily exact such a price: If you take Booth's explanation at face value, his time with the Stones becomes a kind of parable about participatory journalism. The book was a stand-out because Booth involved himself so fully not just in a band tour but in the passions of a generation. And yet, as the world changed, there was no way for that participant to write the book until he became somebody else and could look back on his experience as a thing apart, something that happened to a different person in a time long lost. Either way, the afterword brings me a bit closer to solving the question I asked my editor at Random House, those many years ago. I don't think he knew the answer, anyway.

Jack Schafer

/

TOM WOLFE'S
THE ELECTRIC KOOL-AID ACID TEST

Tom Wolfe writes himself into the second sentence of his book about Ken
Kesey and the Merry Pranksters, *The Electric Kool-Aid Acid Test*, describing
a boaty ride up and down the streets of San Francisco in the open bed of
a Day-Glo-painted pickup truck. It's better than a half-year before 1967's
Summer of Love, and the New York City clotheshorse and leading practi-
tioner of New Journalism looks dowdy compared to the beaded, feathered,
medallioned, and headbanded crew of Kesey associates on board with him.

Wolfe sustains this "you are there" intimacy for the next 400 or so
pages, taking you directly into the heads of his subjects when necessary to
chronicle three years of Prankster adventures in consciousness along the
California coast, across the country in Furthur, their now famous Day-
Gloed 1939 International Harvester school bus, down to Mexico, where
Kesey skedaddled to escape prosecution for possession of marijuana, and
back to San Francisco.

The immediacy is an illusion, because as every Deadhead and tripster
knows, Wolfe was never "on the bus." Yet Wolfe's illusion isn't a false one.
It's a testament to his reportorial skills, which many readers miss because
they're blinded by his bodacious punctuation. "Style can't carry a story if
you haven't done the reporting," Wolfe once attested. As *The Electric Kool-*

Aid Acid Test approaches its fortieth consecutive year in print, it's still the best account—fictional or non, in print or on film—of the genesis of the sixties hipster subculture.

As a raconteur of that culture, Wolfe has competition. Hunter S. Thompson's sensational *Hell's Angels: A Strange and Terrible Saga* (1967), which shares locale and cast with *Acid Test*, introduces the libertine theme that Wolfe's book carries to completion: What possesses people living in a time of unparalleled freedom and a place of unmatched beauty to rebel and demand more? Thompson can't universalize his story because the Hell's Angels were allied with Satan and he didn't really want to in the first place. But Wolfe finds in the Pranksters the germ of a mid-century religious awakening with great potential for universalization, if for no other reason than that the Pranksters were on the side of the angels even though they caroused with the Hell's Angels.

Charles Perry captures the culture of hip in *The Haight-Ashbury: A History* (1984), and the novelists Richard Fariña (*Been Down So Long It Looks Like Up to Me*, 1966) and T. Coraghessan Boyle (*Drop City*, 2003) reflect its spirit. What gives Wolfe the literary leg up on the competition is having a genuine hero—Kesey—who can carry his epic story about the origins of a new culture. Wolfe's Kesey is heroic in the Homeric rather than the tragic sense—manly, clever, a leader, daring, and charismatic. Wolfe's other great book, *The Right Stuff*, similarly exploits a real-life hero, Chuck Yeager, to excellent results. It's no accident that the portraits of Kesey and Yeager are more fully realized than that of any character to be found in Wolfe's fiction. His regard for his heroes has the added benefit of curbing his satirical voice. Satire, even served by a master like Wolfe, is a better spice than main course.

* * *

What makes *The Electric Kool-Aid Acid Test* all the more remarkable is that Wolfe composed its first version on newspaper deadline. It appeared in three installments in January and February 1967 for *New York*, the legendary Sunday magazine of the *New York Herald Tribune* that later would become *New York* Magazine, where he was on staff.

Writing for *New York* and *Esquire* in the sixties was like playing saxophone at the cutting contests at Minton's: You weren't just reporting and writing, you were competing against the likes of Jimmy Breslin, Norman Mailer, Gail Sheehy, Brock Brower, Gay Talese, Terry Southern, and others. These giants were restoring strong narrative, detailed reporting, and point of view to American feature journalism.

The competition extended to editors' offices. At the time, *New York*'s editor, Clay Felker, and Harold Hayes at *Esquire* were rivals for Wolfe's widely acknowledged talents. Wolfe's breakthrough piece, "The Kandy-Kolored Tangerine-Flake Streamline Baby," about custom-car culture, had been assigned to him by *Esquire* during the 1963 New York City newspaper strike. Wolfe claims that he was blocked and that his editor, Byron Dobell, told him to send notes, as the magazine had already committed art and pages to the story. Working in the wee a.m. against the rock 'n' roll soundtrack provided by WABC-AM, Wolfe compiled a hyper memorandum that ran for forty-nine pages. According to the legend provided by Wolfe, Dobell struck the "Dear Byron" at the top and ran the notes as the story.

"Published notes" makes a great tale, so great that Hunter S. Thompson would deploy a variant of it to explain the visceral quality of his feature "The Kentucky Derby Is Decadent and Depraved," but "Kandy-Kolored" doesn't read like any writer's notes I've ever examined. What Wolfe may have discovered was his voice, previously smothered under editors' varnish, and the willingness of editors to take seriously his highbrow, Ph.D.-in-American Studies (Yale) ideas about pop culture in a mass-circulation magazine.

Wolfe intended to fold the Kesey pieces into a future collection of work, but as he commenced to rewrite them he saw the potential of a book. This posed a reportorial problem: The Pranksters had been stoned so much of the time, so who was to say what was true and what was fable? Fortunately there were forty-five hours of film for him to mine that the Pranksters had shot of their Furthur road trips and "acid tests," those psyche-bruising parties in which they commandeered a hall, a club, or a warehouse and apple-seeded California with LSD.

Wolfe also relied on the letters Kesey had sent from Mexico to his friend, the novelist Larry McMurtry, which he used to climb inside the acid king's head. Wolfe was an old hand at mind-meld journalism, having prospected the rock producer Phil Spector's brain in 1964 to describe his panic attack aboard an airplane in "The First Tycoon of Teen." "You really feel you know the person well enough and what their state was in this particular incident or you don't," Wolfe would later say, adding that Spector confirmed the accuracy of the account. "What I try to do is re-create a scene from a triple point of view: the subject's point of view, my own, and that of the other people watching—often within a single paragraph," he said in a 1966 interview.

The Pranksters also offered Wolfe the hours of madcap, reality-bending audio recordings they'd made. He interviewed dozens of Pranksters and Prankster fellow travelers, Kesey's friends from his time at the Stanford University graduate writing program, such as Ed McClanahan and Robert Stone, and he vacuumed up additional tapes and unpublished accounts to get the story. Hunter S. Thompson generously provided interview tapes and other recordings of the Hell's Angels at Kesey's place, explains Marc Weingarten in his valuable new book, *The Gang That Wouldn't Write Straight*. Finally, at a distance from the charismatic Kesey, Wolfe downed 125 micrograms of LSD to learn from the inside what the fuss was all about. His trip was unpleasant, but necessary. "It was like tying yourself to the railroad track and seeing how big the train is, which is rather big," Wolfe said in 1983.

If the magazine pieces were completed on a newspaper deadline, the book was written on a magazine deadline, with Wolfe producing the bulk of it in four intense months, revising in galleys, and publishing it to superlative reviews in August 1968.

Wolfe claims among literary inspirations a band of experimental Soviet writers—the collective "Serapion Brothers," Boris Pilniak, Yevgeni Zamyatin, author of *We*, and others—whom he encountered in the stacks during grad school. "From Zamyatin, I got the idea of the oddly punctuated inner thoughts. I began using a lot of exclamation points and dashes and multiple colons. A lot of dots. The idea was, that's the way people think. People don't think in well-formed sentences," Wolfe told *Rolling Stone* in 1987. The dots and dashes, the all-capital passages, the onomatopoeia ("whirrrrrrrrrrrrrrrrrrr"), the odd ":::::" sequences, and other typographical excesses scar *The Electric Kool-Aid Acid Test* like a bad case of jungle rot. In Wolfe's defense, strong experimentation was called for in a project about LSD culture. As *Acid Test* has remained in print, its stylistic flourishes have become no more outrageous than William Faulkner's similar ambition, never realized, to publish *The Sound and the Fury* using different colored inks to communicate time and event.

* * *

Treating Kesey as a latter-day prophet and the Merry Pranksters as disciples who have discovered a new religion, new sacraments, and gone on the road to spread it could be judged a matter of a writer's Ph.D. overpowering a simpler tale about a group of founding stoners. "If there was ever a group devoted totally to the here and now it was the Pranksters," Wolfe writes in *Acid Test*. "I remember puzzling over this. There was something so . . . religious in the air, in the very atmosphere of the Prankster life, and yet one couldn't put one's finger on it." But by the time Wolfe describes Kesey and the Pranksters practically taking over a Unitarian retreat to which they had been invited and nearly driving the Unitarians and their children to religion, you begin to believe.

Of course, Kesey and the Pranksters didn't single-handedly invent psychedelic culture, and they weren't the only LSD proselytizers in the mid-sixties. Timothy Leary instructed his followers to drop acid in a quiet room, escape the material world, and merge with the godhead. The Pranksters, on the other hand, swung the big broom, sweeping everything into their acid gospel—trash and kitsch, consumer culture, spray paint, electronics, daredevilry, and practical jokes, and it was their version that rose to dominance. Young people in San Francisco, then California, then around the world followed their template: The Pranksters literally wore the flag, which would become a cliché by 1969, if not before; they imagined themselves comic-book heroes; romanticized the American Indian; playfully taunted the straights; and danced all night as they immersed themselves in the mixed-media salad of rock music, tape-recorder feedback loops, whirling movie cameras, strobe lights, and cosmic light shows.

Whether the Prankster notions about how best to experience and interpret psychedelic drugs ascended because they were the optimum prescription or simply because Wolfe's best-selling report immediately achieved canonical status in every college town, high school, and dirt-road hamlet—wherever young people wanted to get high and drive—can't be teased apart. *Doonesbury's* cartoonist, Garry Trudeau, for one, lifted the name of Merry Prankster Steve "Zonker" Lambrecht and gave it to the Pranksteresque acidhead in his strip. Just as Jack Kerouac's *On the Road* inspires folks to hitchhike the country, Wolfe's book still provides map and route for modern explorers of internal space. What's the annual Burning Man festival—with all its costumes, modern pharmaceuticals, spacey music, bright lights, and tribal noise—but a grander, updated acid test?

If all journalism is autobiography, there's a fair bit of Wolfe in his portrait of Ken Kesey, the outsider, challenger of the literary establishment, and failed movement leader. Almost a decade before Wolfe declared his school of narrative-powered New Journalism as the successor to the novel and about two decades before Wolfe heeded his own call for the return of the reported novel by publishing *Bonfire of the Vanities*, Kesey had produced two reported works of fiction, 1962's *One Flew Over the Cuckoo's Nest* and 1964's *Sometimes a Great Notion.* The antiunion message of *Sometimes a Great Notion*, which glorifies strike-breaking loggers, makes the reactionary journalism of Wolfe's "Radical Chic," in which he lampooned a Leonard Bernstein benefit for the Black Panthers, seem like a Ripon Society pamphlet in comparison. Wolfe encouraged the comparison to Kesey in 1989 by rejecting the conservative and reactionary labels, telling the *Paris Review* he preferred being called a "seer."

While both Kesey and Wolfe had their visions, neither turned out to be much of a seer. The New Journalism didn't replace the novel, as the somewhat messianic Wolfe later predicted it would in 1973's *The New Journalism*, and Wolfe's successes with the reported novel haven't been widely imitated. Kesey, who abandoned the novel to stage drug-aided real-time dramas with the Pranksters, failed to take the psychedelic movement through the next "door" by going "beyond acid," i.e., to a place where drugs weren't needed. He wrote very little noteworthy fiction or nonfiction after *Sometimes a Great Notion.* He seems to have lost his bearings in the process of rising from literary fame to celebrity, which Wolfe describes in *Acid Test.* It would be fair to say the transformation from fame to celebrity has fatigued Wolfe too.

* * *

Like many forty-year-olds, *The Electric Kool-Aid Acid Test* carries a wad of fat around its midriff that could be pruned without harming the body. Modern readers can scan the portions set like poetry without missing much. There's a sameness to many of the Prankster adventures—Hey, somebody else's acid trip can never be as interesting as your own!—and the book stalls for me when Kesey goes to Mexico. But as I recall reading the book when it was still green, when Kesey and acid and Owsley and The Grateful Dead and psychedelia were still au courant, it hummed along with remarkable economy.

Far from inspiring a legion of journalists to renew the craft, Wolfe mostly—and quite inadvertently—spawned two generations' worth of boneheads who thought the lesson of New Journalism was to pound on the exclamation key while writing yourself into the story. He also became the scapegoat for journalistic scandal and excess—from Janet Cooke (the *Los Angeles Times* media critic David Shaw did the finger-pointing) to Bob Woodward's indulgent "you are there" scenes.

This is a little like blaming The Beatles for The Monkees. Had Wolfe never pushed the stylistic boundaries, we'd still be acknowledging his career-long knack for discovering cultural trends and making sense of them. It ain't an easy beat. The Department of Commerce doesn't publish quarterly statistics showing a rise in religious yearning, a spike in surf culture, or a growing societal trend of self-obsession that a cultural reporter can plot and graph.

As the Bible and many lesser books show, narrative is the finest container ever devised to transport ideas, especially transporting ideas over time. Forty years from now, when Wolfe's book, I predict, will still be in print, our grandchildren will be celebrating his role in resuscitating the narrative form. They'll marvel at his hacklike abilities to get just enough of the hard-to-get portions of the acid legend to tell the complete story with authority. And they'll be carrying a copy of *The Electric Kool-Aid Acid Test* in their hip pockets.

Naresh Fernandes

PALAGUMMI SAINATH'S
EVERYBODY LOVES A GOOD DROUGHT: STORIES FROM INDIA'S POOREST DISTRICTS

One evening, a couple of summers ago, *The Times of India* organized a free classical music concert at an amphitheater cut into a hill along Bombay's coast. It was a stunning locale, with the sea in the distance and twinkling stars overhead. All around the stage, giant canvases depicted idyllic scenes of a futuristic Bombay—a city whose contemporary counterpart is an urban nightmare so disturbing, it is the object of intense study by planners and social scientists from around the world. More than 55 percent of the city's 13 million residents live in slums, while poorly built drainage systems leave even newly constructed office districts flooded after heavy rains. But in *The Times of India*'s utopian vision, Bombay was bathed in the colors of sunset, as birds swooped amid glass-and-steel buildings. To the immediate right of the musicians, for instance, was an enormous image of the completed Bandra Worli Sea Link, a bridge that is being built across an inlet of the Arabian Sea. When it is ready—though no one is sure when exactly that will be—city administrators hope the Sea Link will speed the crawl from the suburbs to the southern office districts. Rush-hour traffic in Bombay now moves at less than 12 kilometers an hour.

Before the musicians could really get going, the marketing manager of *The Times*—which claims to be the best-selling English-language broadsheet in the world—came out to rally the audience. "Do you believe we have the potential to become a world-class city?" she shouted. The crowd of middle-class Bombay residents bellowed its assent, unmindful of the fact that when the Bandra Worli Sea Link is complete, it will conduct thousands of honking, roaring cars and trucks within 150 meters of the venue in which they were sitting, making music performances (and even lingering conversations) impossible. More alarming, environmentalists believe that the Sea Link was directly responsible for many of the 452 deaths that resulted from a freak cloudburst in 2005: the construction of the bridge narrowed the mouth of a vital drainage channel that flows into the bay, making it incapable of handling the heavy rain and causing a flood upstream that inundated several neighborhoods along the banks of the channel.

The audience's enthusiastic approval of the dubious suggestion that Bombay (which I prefer to the official name, Mumbai) stands on the brink of greatness was just another indication of the cocoon of willful ignorance in which India's middle and upper classes have chosen to seclude themselves when it comes to their country's economic situation. This sliver of India's population—estimated at 200 million people—has disproportionately enjoyed the benefits of the country's 9 percent surge of economic growth in recent years, and is now among the most courted groups of consumers on the planet. It has grabbed the attention of producers of so-called FMCGs, or "fast-moving consumer goods," from around the world. Even luxury brands such as Gucci and Louis Vuitton have set up shop in India, encouraged by the fact that the country is home to the world's fourth-largest number of billionaires. All the cheerleading about India's future, though, ignores the reality that a full 77 percent of the country's population of just over 1.1 billion is struggling on less than 50 cents a day. While a tiny percentage of the population, mainly in the cities, enjoys a level of affluence unimaginable a generation ago, rural India—home to more than 70 percent of the country's population—is wracked by a man-made agricultural crisis that has driven nearly 150,000 farmers to commit suicide between 1997 and 2005, the latest year for which figures are available. But such stories find relatively little space in most of India's English-language newspapers and on television news shows, which are the primary sources of news and information for the country's urban elite. (Hindi is the national language, but most businessmen, senior bureaucrats, the higher courts, and the best universities use English. While Hindi- and regional-language newspapers often cover stories about the countryside more intensely, their increasingly local focus, facilitated by new technology that allows narrowly zoned editions, means that these issues are rarely seen from a national perspective.)

The journalist Palagummi Sainath says this growing economic gulf between India's elite and the vast majority of its population has created a similar disconnect "between mass media and mass reality." Sainath, now the rural affairs editor of *The Hindu*, one of the few remaining English-language broadsheets devoted to serious journalism, is the author of *Everybody Loves a Good Drought: Stories from India's Poorest Districts*, perhaps the most admired collection of reportage to have been published in India in the last two decades. His series of meticulously reported articles about the lives of India's most underprivileged was written between May 1993 and June 1995 (the articles were collected in a book in 1996), soon after the country began to restructure its economy in accordance with the prescriptions of free-market advocates. But even that early in the so-called "liberalization" process, it was clear that the withdrawal of agricultural subsidies and ill-considered budget cuts were causing great distress in a country that is still overwhelmingly rural. Rereading *Everybody Loves a Good Drought* today is a startling reminder of how much English-language journalism has changed in India—and how quickly. Today, it's difficult to imagine most broadsheets investing so much money or devoting quite so much space to stories that don't directly relate to their "TG," or target group, an ungainly piece of marketing jargon that is commonly used in many newsrooms as a synonym for "reader."

Though the crisis in the countryside has only grown since Sainath wrote *Drought*, forcing millions of farmers to abandon their plots and seek employment in cities, many of India's English-language newspapers are transforming themselves into halls of mirrors, focusing only on news that they believe will interest their elite readers. This metamorphosis is the product both of a perfervid neoliberal climate in which everything, including the news, has become a commodity that's up for sale, and of a generational shift in newspaper ownership.

As in many parts of the world, India's newspapers are family-owned and run. In the four decades after independence in 1947, many of the proprietors were content to let journalists make the decisions about editorial content. This relatively hands-off approach was a legacy of the freedom struggle, which nationalist newspapers had shaped and help to sustain. But since the 1990s, a new generation of newspaper owners has adopted a number-crunching approach to journalism. Many of them view the news merely as the stuff between the ads. In some cases, they've even attempted to ensure that the editorial content is designed to create an environment that's conducive to attracting advertising. Taking this attitude to the extreme, *The Times of India* has set up a unit called Medianet that actually sells editorial space to advertisers. With uncharacteristic coyness, the unit's Web site says that it provides "comprehensive media coverage and content solutions to clients."

So while the readers of India's English-language newspapers are served supplements with titles like *Splurge*, in which they can learn all about holidays in Monaco and the latest yachts, they are denied the information they need to understand how projects like the Bandra Worli Sea Link or the upheaval on the country's farms are affecting their lives.

The Times of India, which claims a readership of approximately 1.7 million in Bombay and 6.8 million countrywide, has advocated the concept of "aspirational journalism." The paper, for which I once worked, is now run by Samir Jain and his brother, Vineet. They have often told their journalists that the *Times* must help readers forget the mundane reality of their lives and show them the possibilities of what their new affluence can bring. Famously, Samir Jain once ordered his journalists in Bombay to stop reporting on the garbage that frequently is left uncollected in the city's streets because of inefficient city administrators. "Our readers have difficult lives," he told me at the only meeting I ever had with him. "We should put a smile to their faces every morning instead of reminding them of their problems."

Jain's enormously profitable publication has set an example that many other newspapers have followed. Many of India's English-language newspapers have abandoned the responsibility of being the fourth pillar of democracy (a role that many of them had first begun to embrace during the struggle for independence against the British). Now, they claim that they are mere content providers devoted to delivering to advertisers the largest number of eyeballs possible. As a result, the increasing divide between rich and poor that is a consequence of new economic policies introduced in the early 1990s—which include a predilection for privatizing even profitable public enterprises and slashing subsidies in several sectors, including health and education—is not really part of the public discourse.

Meanwhile, India ranks 128th on the United Nations' human-development index (which measures life expectancy, educational standards, and standard of living), below such economic tigers as the Dominican Republic, Bolivia, and Guatemala. The themes around which *Everybody Loves a Good Drought* is organized—debt, health, education, displacement, irrigation—remain the biggest problems India must tackle if it is to improve the lives of *all* its citizens. Yet despite the obvious problems, large sections of the country's English-language press operate as though they are allies of the state in a national project to convince citizens that India is predestined to soar to global supremacy. That sentiment was highlighted in a recent *Times of India* advertising campaign that had as its punch line the phrase, "India Poised," suggesting that the nation stood on the precipice of imminent greatness. (Ironically, it was the *Times* that first published Sainath's searing reportage that eventually became *Drought*. In fact, the newspaper gave him a fellowship to fund his research, when the father of the present owners was chairman of the company.)

I first met Sainath in 1992, when he wrote a column called "The Last Page" for *Blitz*, a left-wing tabloid that was then wavering in its political principles. Each week, his column would tackle a wildly varying subject— the injustice of international patent law, the absurdity of the government's agrarian policies, the hypocrisies of the Hindu fundamentalist Bharatiya Janata Party—with the delicate wit and insight that would later characterize *Drought*. I'd already heard about his legendary charisma: Sainath had taught a journalism class at a local women's college for several years, and after they graduated, his awestruck students would gush about his talent during tea breaks in newsrooms across the country. He won the *Times* fellowship and went out on the road shortly after I made his acquaintance, but by then he'd already encouraged me to expand the range of my reading (he introduced me to Gunnar Myrdal's *Asian Drama* and later gifted me a copy of Graham Hancock's *Lords of Poverty*), and left me with the realization that poverty needed to be reported as a process, not as a series of glaring events, such as starvation deaths or famine.

Magnitude is among India's defining characteristics, and Indian journalists are often overwhelmed by—and myopically focused on—the statistics and those glaring events. (Consider that half of all Indian children under four are malnourished, the number of illiterate Indians today is larger than the country's total population when it won independence, and one of every three people in the world suffering from tuberculosis is Indian). But in *Everybody Loves a Good Drought*, Sainath brings to life the tragedies that lurk in the gray print of official reports: he shows us the structural reasons for poverty. Few Indian journalists had undertaken the kind of rigorous reporting trips that he had, even in the preliberalization period, when journalism that sought out the view from society's margins was a much more valued endeavor. Sainath traveled more than 80,000 bumpy kilometers through the country's 10 poorest districts—the basic administrative units that comprise India's states—to learn how the country's poor survive during the 200–240 days after the spring and winter crops have been harvested, when there is no agricultural work to be had.

The coping strategies he found were astonishing. As he writes, "Some of them [are] quite ingenious, all of them back-breaking." In Godda, in the northern state of Bihar, Sainath followed a man named Kishan Yadav on a 60-kilometer journey as the laborer pushed a reinforced bicycle piled with 250 kilograms of low-grade coal scavenged from the waste dumps of mines all the way to the market. The three-day ordeal, repeated twice a week, was how 3,000 men in the district kept their families alive—a miracle, it would seem, because they earned only about 10 rupees (about 25 cents at the time) a day. In Ramnad, in the southern state of Tamil Nadu, Sainath spent time with 27-year-old Ratnapandi Nadar, who eked out a living tapping palm trees for sap that could be boiled into a sweetener called "jaggery." Nadar worked a 16-hour day that began at three in the morning, climbing at least 40 trees. "That is roughly equivalent to walking up and down a building of 250 floors daily, using the staircase," notes Sainath.

In a country where poverty is depressingly visible all the time, many middle-class Indians have developed blinders to the distress around them. Sainath's great achievement was to make readers start to pay attention to their poorer countrymen. His lucid writing, so evident in these powerful portraits, had much to do with this. Too often, reportage on poverty is unremittingly grim, weighed down by a severity that deters all but the most determined readers. But *Everybody Loves a Good Drought*, in addition to being marked by a profound empathy for its subjects, is leavened with black humor. That quality is especially on display when Sainath describes the absurd theater of poverty-alleviation programs and the industry that has sprung up to help "uplift" the less fortunate, to use a verb frequently employed by Indian bureaucrats.

Among the pieces that best illustrate this tragicomedy is a story from Naupada in Orissa, in which Sainath tells of Mangal Sunani's delight when the government gifted him a cow as part of a poverty-reduction scheme. Officials told Sunani that he and scores of others in the district (who were also given cows) would prosper after their animals were impregnated with the semen of a Jersey bull, thereby producing high-yield cows and other bulls. The officials even gave Sunani an acre of land for free, so that he could grow fodder for the cattle, and offered to pay him the minimum daily wage to work the plot. To ensure that the cows didn't accidentally mate with a local bull, all the male cattle in the region were castrated.

Two years later, the community only had eight crossbred calves; many other calves had died shortly after they were born because the crossbred cows were susceptible to disease. By then, the local, hardier species of cattle had been wiped out because of the castration drive and the cow herders were forced to buy milk from the market. When they attempted to grow vegetables on the patches of land they'd been given, officials were annoyed: they wouldn't be paid their wage if they raised anything but fodder, the villagers were warned. Sainath dryly headlined the piece, VERY FEW SPECIMENS—BUT A LOT OF BULL.

The ludicrousness of the situation even creeps into the names of some of the places from which the dispatches have been filed. One report is from a region of Orissa state that is officially called Cut-Off Area, home to the residents of 152 villages who are stranded on islands in a reservoir created by a dam built in the 1960s to generate hydroelectricity. Though these villagers saw their farms submerged when the power project was constructed, almost none of them actually has electricity at home. Sainath points out that between 1951 and 1990, more than 26 million Indians have been displaced by development projects. But the rewards of these dams, canals, and mines have rarely trickled down to the so-called beneficiaries. It's a section of the book that has special resonance today, given that the Indian government has recently approved the creation of close to 400 Special Economic Zones, which has resulted in even more farmers being pressured to sell off their land cheaply. The government hopes to attract more investment by giving firms that open offices in the SEZs incentives such as tax holidays and flexible labor regulations. As of early October 2007, just over 500 square kilometers had been acquired for these zones. In *Drought*,

Sainath writes, "If the costs [the poor] bear are the price of development, then the rest of the nation is having a free lunch."

Driven by the conviction that, as he suggests, "the press can and does make a difference when it functions" because "governments do react and respond" to reportage, Sainath's commitment to telling the stories of the neglected was obvious from his enormous personal investment in *Drought*: his fellowship grant was too small to match his ambition, so he kicked in all his retirement savings. Ironically, by the time the pieces were finally collected as a book in 1996, the business managers who had wrested control of newsrooms from the journalists weren't interested in supporting this kind of journalism. Though the book had fired the imaginations of young journalists across India, almost no publications have been willing to invest the resources necessary to allow lengthy investigations into the causes—or processes—of poverty and deprivation. (Today, only *The Hindu*, its sister publication, *Frontline* magazine, and *Tehelka*, a weekly magazine, seem to regularly find the space for stories about the millions who have been left behind by India's economic surge.) Nonetheless, the book earned Sainath a string of awards both at home and abroad. He has used some of the money he's received from these awards to establish fellowships for rural reporters, giving journalists in small towns who write in regional languages the opportunity and the training to more effectively tell the stories of the countryside. For his part, Sainath, now fifty, continues to write for *The Hindu* about the economic forces that have pushed thousands of debt-ridden farmers to commit suicide in recent years.

In the last chapter of the book, Sainath considers the role the press could play in promoting genuine development in India. He notes that even when rural stories do find their way into the newspapers, journalists often tend to turn the nongovernmental agencies that have proliferated across the subcontinent into heroes, even though their strategies are often suspect. Covering development "calls for placing people and their needs at the centre of the stories. Not any intermediaries, however saintly," he stresses. He also suggests journalists must begin to pay more attention to rural "political action and class conflict," even at the risk of being labeled leftist. "Evading reality helps no one," he writes. "A society that does not know itself cannot cope."

But that's unlikely to happen as newspapers devote their attention to providing infotainment to consumers, rather than news to citizens.

Nonetheless, readers of *The Times of India* were pleasantly surprised a few months ago to wake up to a new advertising campaign for the newspaper featuring the subcontinent's most famous film star, Amitabh Bachchan, admitting that the burst of economic growth had failed to benefit the country's poorest. "There are two Indias in this country," he declared in a television commercial shot on the contentious Bandra Worli Sea Link.

However, Bachchan's scriptwriter had a novel take on the crisis: he blamed the poor for preventing India from realizing its true potential. As he potters around the 5.6-kilometer bridge, Bachchan says, "One India is straining at the leash, eager to spring forth and live up to all the adjectives that the world has been recently showering upon us. The other India is the leash."

At the end of the long spot (which runs two minutes, thirteen seconds), Bachchan declares, "The ride has brought us to the edge of time's great precipice. And one India—a tiny little voice at the back of the head—is looking down at the bottom of the ravine and hesitating. The other India is looking up at the sky and saying, 'It's time to fly.'" Bachchan then strides off purposefully across the bridge, even though the middle span hasn't been constructed yet. But the camera, as is often the case these days, doesn't follow him to his logical end.

Chris Lehmann

CHARLES RAW, BRUCE PAGE, & GODFREY HODGSON'S
DO YOU SINCERELY WANT TO BE RICH?

As any follower of the grim judicial endgame of the Enron affair knows, the investment world can morph, at its speculative outer limit, into an empire of sandcastles. Fabulous sums of shareholder value wash away with the brutal ebb tide of a market correction, and before you know it, some $60 billion in, shareholder value and employee pensions are good and sunk.

The real wonder, though, is how the financial press keeps missing the casual brigandry of the Kenneth Lays, Jeffrey Skillings, and Andrew Fastows in real time. Business writers had, after all, designated Enron the poster company for the brave new age of energy deregulation, routinely hymning its many market wonders until a *Fortune* scribe named Bethany McLean—thanks to a tip from a short-seller—noticed the distinct scent of eyewash arising from the company's 2001 money prospectus. And so it has been with other failed and flailing wonder speculators, from Tyco and Imclone all the way back to the 1920s Florida real-estate bubble.

Whenever a speculative enterprise swerves confidently into fairyland, reporters tag along to marvel uncritically at the view; and whenever said enterprise crashes to the ground, it is just as credulously treated as something entirely new under the sun. To save embarrassment all around, these speculative collapses are subsequently treated as the handiwork of but a few greedy, misguided, or delusional bad actors. Like Messrs. Lay, Skilling, and Fastow, they may pay their individual criminal debt to society, but they will studiously stiff their employees and shareholders with the bulk of their paper-generated ruination, as press observers look on with tacit, self-flattering disdain for the many poor suckers drawn into the disastrous wake of it all. If the informal motto of the American financial press atop a bubble is "What, me worry?" it becomes, when conditions of financial gravity are restored, "Rubes? Who, us?"

All of which makes the reappearance of *Do You Sincerely Want to Be Rich?* a splendid market correction in its own right. First published in 1971, the book is the fruit of some five years' worth of dogged investigative work from Charles Raw, Bruce Page, and Godfrey Hodgson of *The Sunday Times* of London. *Do You Sincerely Want to Be Rich?* is a financial farce worthy of Nathaniel West, or perhaps David Mamet on acid. It is, in short, an exhaustive study of one of the strangest financial success stories of the swinging 1960s, Bernie Cornfeld's Investors Overseas Services.

Raw, Page, and Hodgson attend with admirable clarity to the many fathomless mysteries of IOS balance sheets and their sweeping vistas of releveraged debt, but they also painstakingly reconstruct the go-go money culture of the 1960s that made such a mad enterprise possible. Just as important in a book often thick with forensic accounting detail, they relate the crazed IOS chronicle in an engaging narrative tone of stolid empirical bewilderment, nicely captured in chapter subheads composed in the voice of satirical Victorian novels: "in which respectable financiers strip off their watch chains and leap into the warm offshore waters. . . . IOS, on the basis of a very curious prospectus, becomes a public corporation at long last." In all these respects—though most of all by virtue of the principled reporterly skepticism in which the authors told the IOS tale, in both real time and retrospect—*Do You Sincerely Want to Be Rich?* is a model of lively financial writing that journalistic specialists would do well to study and emulate.

* * *

IOS was a financial colossus entirely suited to its age. Toward the end of the postwar investing boom, stockbrokers boasted that they were "gunslingers" and began to herd investors accordingly into visions of higher investor returns and lower tax rates in far-off lands, well beyond the grid of square, flatfoot regulators such as the Securities and Exchange Commission.

Bernie Cornfeld was in many ways the age's premier gunslinger—certainly a spur-jangling pioneer in an investing scene still dominated by blue-chip brokerages. Though Cornfeld gave precious little thought to the notion at the time, when he first alighted in Paris in 1955, alongside all sorts of other misfit American expats, he was launching a new phase in the accelerating modern wonder of mobile capital. It was the moment when money could functionally secede from nationhood; indeed, as it continued sprawling across the globe, IOS assumed the character of a cash-rich antistate, a collection of offshore transactions that, as the authors write, "should be as far as possible untaxed, unregulated, and uncontrolled." This meant that IOS fund managers were sort of colonial bottom feeders, erecting their counterempire "out of the juridical anomalies left over by the Holy Roman Empire and the colonial systems of Spain, the Netherlands and Great Britain." For all of the fund's hectically advertised market sophistication, the reasoning behind IOS's global growth was baby simple, the authors write: Since investment regulations took root in the aftermath of a global depression, they mirror the belief of every Western government "that uncontrolled financial speculation is a danger to the stability of the State. Ultimately, what IOS did was to get around virtually every control designed to prevent speculation getting out of hand."

IOS was a pioneer of the offshore franchise, and true to its founding vision, it routinely repurposed its corporate identity so as to better exploit those spots around the globe that offered minimal regulation and/or law enforcement. A few years after Cornfeld launched the fund, IOS had to hotfoot it out of France when the authorities wanted to restrict its postal privileges. Cornfeld promptly shifted operations to Switzerland, but eventually ran afoul of that corporate paradise when the Swiss authorities began lusting after the fund's incorporation revenues. (Cornfeld, of course, had procured for IOS a "brass plate address" in Panama, where it could operate virtually tax-free.) Rather than relinquish those tax breaks to the Swiss, Cornfeld actually split his home office and moved half of it back to France, while also maintaining a Swiss arm mainly for the prestige value it offered IOS sales reps as they courted global investors who wanted all manner of financial secrecy to conceal all manner of financial trespasses against their home-nation laws.

IOS's chosen vehicle was the comparatively new financial instrument known as the mutual fund. The singular inspiration of IOS was to wed the flexibility of mutual funds to a globalizing investment community just beginning to stir to a fitful recognition of its own potential might. In short order, IOS went from being a minor franchise of a New York-based mutual fund into a hydraheaded financial shape-shifter, built on little more than the simple idea of liquid capital. It could be virtually all things to all people. In the new global financial frontier, it could become a de facto investment bank, putting together a takeover of a British-based aircraft conglomerate. It could play at real-estate moguldom, lining up eurodollars and petrodollars to erect retirement condominium settlements in Florida. Or it could become a freebooting arbitrageur of spectacularly bad judgment, as when it took over an unsightly corporate hybrid known as Commonwealth United Corporation, which began life as a jukebox manufacturer, managed to couple with an insurance agency and a film studio, before acquiring a cash-devouring California oil concern far past its prime, and dying unceremoniously amid a desperate effort to kite a whole wheelbarrow full of credit via the rights to a Julie Andrews musical movie, *Darling Lili.* Hey, it was the sixties, okay?

Cornfeld—along with his main associate gunslinger, a Harvard Law-credentialed highflier named Edward M. Cowett—kept the con running with voguish pronouncements of the financial revolution that IOS was midwifing across the globe. Hodgson, Raw, and Page bring a proper note of horrified fascination to their portrait of Cornfeld. They recognize that, much as IOS serves up a parable on the follies of unregulated capitalism without borders, Cornfeld was a veritable random search engine for bullshit theories of social leveling through investment.

To be sure, there had been a good deal of placid trickle-down booster-ism in the market boom of the 1920s, whose essence was neatly distilled in the General Motors executive John J. Raskob's 1929 *Ladies' Home Journal* essay "Everybody Ought to Be Rich." But the IOS credo, quoted in the title of Raw, Page, and Hodgson's corporate biography, sported more than just the whiff of 1960s-era authenticity. In his more hectic, prophetic moments, Cornfeld cast himself as a vessel of full-blown social revolution. A former Socialist Youth League member who campaigned for the Socialist Party presidential candidate Norman Thomas and graduated from college with a degree in social work, Cornfeld routinely touted his bundle of mutual funds as a heroic blow struck against the brittle oligarchy of The Man, on behalf of the Common Investor. "World-Wide People's Capitalism" was the struggle he celebrated, and his rhetoric took on a glow that the authors describe as "positively Messianic": "'The service we perform is vital not only to our economic system,'" Cornfeld preached, "'but in a real sense it contributes to the survival of the democratic process.'"

Cornfeld's success was as striking for the character of his sales force as it was for the ripe military clientele they approached. He recruited his first cohort of salesmen from among the American expat community. In the Paris of the 1950s, as the authors write, this was "a tolerant society: a mildly Bohemian life-style was expected, and some vague stirring of political radicalism was almost demanded. It was a world of frustrated intellectuals, mild neurotics, political nonconformists, and cultural misfits—with the occasional drunk or homosexual." Conceptual salesman that he was, Cornfeld's other breakthrough was to mint these wayward souls into an echt-sixties sales force, versed in the motivational psychology that freed Cornfeld, a veteran of a number of encounter groups devoted to Alfred Adler's "rational therapy" movement, of his stateside neuroses. This reclamation project was likely a fulfillment of a "deep need" of Cornfeld's own, the authors write, "for it carried the promise that his recruits would become devoted followers of the man who could perform an act of liberation for them. In the beginning, Investors Overseas Services sometimes seemed more like a therapeutic community than a money-making device."

An ancillary but far from negligible virtue of *Do You Sincerely Want to Be Rich?* is that it supplies a much-needed corrective to the stubborn mythology of the 1960s as an idealistic near-utopian era of cultural radicalism, in which the counterculture was by definition also countermaterialistic. The strange career of IOS points up very much the opposite trend, in which liberated nouveau bohemian salesmen racked up absurdly inflated fees and rewarded themselves with lavish homes, vehicles, and retinues of models—all on the example of Great Leader Cornfeld, who commanded at the height of the IOS scam a genuine Swiss villa and his own jet. So tightly does the IOS saga merge the money culture and the let-it-all-hang-out dogma of sixties liberationism that *Do You Sincerely Want to Be Rich?* often reads like an extended finance-world appendix to Thomas Frank's study of the sixties "creative revolution" in American advertising, *The Conquest of Cool.* In both Frank's saga and this one, one appreciates that the jargon of maximum liberation was little more than a fig leaf concealing the hoary quest for Croesus-like excess.

Yet the quest for all manner of ultrahip, ultraglobal gratification turned back in on itself in curious ways, as IOS continued pursuing the main moneyed chance wherever it might lead. For one thing, the great wide world of investing proved on inspection to be disconcertingly small, especially when it came to the range of motion available to the masters of the IOS universe once they ran out of options.

For another, great wealth seems always and everywhere to confer an equally great longing for cultural respectability. So as IOS acquired its far-flung isthmus of extralegal offshore investments—ranging from Africa to South America to the Middle East—it also hotly coveted an image as a clearinghouse for great charitable pursuits, deep public thoughts, and the eminent personages who make all such things happen. Via a friendship with Barney Rosset, president of Grove Press, Cornfeld was able to engineer a most ironic coup by recruiting James Roosevelt—the eldest son of the president who created IOS's great institutional nemesis, the Securities and Exchange Commission—to serve on the IOS board. Roosevelt *fils* was also to act, more informally, as a troubleshooting ambassador of good will to the many nations where IOS found itself running afoul of the law or the ruling financier class.

Then there was Pacem in Terris, the global peace conference that IOS sponsored in its highest-flying phase. The authors dub it, most accurately, a "solemn farce" involving representatives convened from seventy different nations at Geneva's swank Intercontinental hotel on May 28, 1970. Among its other difficulties, the authors note, the peace-themed gathering "coincided with a resumption of American bombing in Vietnam and with the outbreak of the Six-Day War in the Middle East." Among the assembled unwitting luminaries were John Kenneth Galbraith, Senator William Fulbright, a Swiss cardinal, and the editor of *Le Monde*. (Galbraith was able to serve up some delayed rehabilitation to his reputation by lavishly praising *Do You Sincerely Want to Be Rich?* upon its original release in a review for *The Washington Post*.)

The great day of disillusionment came in 1969, shortly after IOS floated its initial public offering, a move that is hard to square with any notion of consensual financial reality. For IPOs are the great invitation for shareholders of all descriptions to cash in—to redeem plentiful stock shares as other investors rally to capitalize a growing company. But IOS was not, by then, really growing at all. Fully $8 million of the $52 million raised in the

IPO went instantly to shareholder redemptions, meaning that IOS was quite literally mortgaging its future against its rapidly contracting present. Cornfeld's frantic right-hand man Cowett promptly launched a clandestine, and probably illegal, campaign to buy up some $11 million in IPO shares in an effort to keep the stock price—launched at $10 a share—artificially high.

It failed. Global stock markets were contracting in 1969 anyway, and IOS was at the most exposed edge of every sort of market imaginable. Cornfeld and his corporate board still prayed for deliverance in the form of a deal with John McCandish King, a Denver-based financier who made his millions in exploiting tax breaks to oil investors—and producing precious little black gold in the process. Indeed, the IPO, in its most fundamental particulars, was a tissue of lies, placing IOS profits at $25 million for 1969—$10 million of which being purely speculative returns from King's forever-speculative oil holdings. Later inquiries disclosed that more than $7 million of that figure was fed into shell-game-style loans among IOS board members to leverage hot new acquisitions that usually went into their own profit-challenged deep freezes upon acquisition. An adjusted audit would show a $10.2 million profit, the authors write—and nearly all of that in the highly hypothetical form of paper profits on King's oil fields; take that away, Hodgson, Raw, and Page reckoned, and the company made "virtually nothing" in the big breakout year of 1969. A somewhat more sober reckoning came courtesy of the one honest accountant on the scene, Mel Lechner, who announced a still-optimistic $17.9 million profit in 1969—and losses of between $7 million and $13 million in the first half of 1970 alone.

Once those unforgiving numbers surfaced, the stock tanked, and board members voted Cornfeld out of his leadership post. They also approved a takeover bid from King, but SEC rules barred him from the position. So in 1970, control of IOS passed to the takeover magnate Robert Vesco, who would later gain no small renown as the bankroller of some of Richard Nixon's shadier extramural initiatives. Vesco would eventually be accused of embezzling more than $200 million from IOS funds, and then launched his own expat career to avoid SEC prosecution. He is now serving a long sentence in a Cuban prison.

All of which makes a fitting epitaph for an investment empire founded originally on the giddy bohemian quest for the global main chance. It's also a critical reminder—one among many in this absorbing, sprawling saga of delusional chicanery on a worldwide scale—that the follies of the past link up directly to the crimes of successive ages. We do well to ponder such matters as we await the Enron verdict, and its attendant official assurances that the slate is wiped clean, that American markets need never fear the accession of another Ken Lay. With *Do You Sincerely Want to Be Rich?* finally back in print, we should have less reason than ever to buy into that speculative forecast.

Connie Schultz

—

MICHAEL HERR'S
DISPATCHES

In the fall of 1978, I was racing through Kent State University's campus bookstore when a thin book, propped in a section where it didn't belong, stopped me in my tracks. The cover was the color of a brown paper bag, with a one-word title in headline type at the top: *Dispatches*. A single blurb, by John le Carré, appeared beneath the title: "The best book I have ever read on men and war in our time."

In our time. It had to be about Vietnam. I looked at the bottom for the author's name: Michael Herr. Never heard of him. I turned to the first chapter, called "Breathing In," and started to read its italicized beginning:

> *There was a map of Vietnam on the wall of my apartment in Saigon and some nights, coming back late to the city, I'd lie out on my bed and look at it, too tired to do anything more than just get my boots off. That map was a marvel, especially now that it wasn't real anymore.*

I deposited my notebooks on the floor, let my purse slide off my shoulder to join them.

> *If dead ground could come back and haunt you the way dead people do, they'd have been able to mark my map current and burn the ones they'd been using since '64, but count on it, nothing like that was going to hap-*

pen. It was late '67 now, even the most detailed maps didn't reveal much anymore; reading them was like trying to read the faces of the Vietnamese, and that was like trying to read the wind. We knew that the uses of most information were flexible, different pieces of ground told different stories to different people. We also knew that for years now there had been no country here but the war.

I don't remember how much I read before I bought *Dispatches*. Fellow asthmatics will likely understand why, more than thirty years later, I can still easily remember shorter and shorter breaths, working myself up to a low-grade wheeze by the time I came to the nonitalicized text on the fourth page: "A couple of rounds fired off in the dark a kilometer away and the Elephant would be there kneeling on my chest, sending me down into my boots for a breath."

The image of that elephant forces a palm to my chest even now, reminding me to breathe. Perhaps that is where I stopped reading in 1978, and decided to take the book home, where I wouldn't be surrounded by strangers.

Issues that push and pull at us in equal measure are the ones mostly likely to haunt us. Vietnam was, and is, one of those ghosts for me—because of my roots, not my politics. Ohio, where I grew up, ranked fifth in the number of war casualties in Vietnam. Twenty-six of the servicemen who died came from my home county of Ashtabula, which was full of farmers who hoped to hand off the land to their sons, and working-class boys hoping to graduate from high school and follow their dads into factories that produced rubber, steel, and automobiles. But hope took a holiday in neighborhoods like ours during the war. By the late 1960s, it seemed you couldn't drive three blocks in any direction without passing the house of a boy who had gone to Vietnam. Neighbors would take over potluck and beer the night before these boys boarded the first flights of their lives. They left full of brag and bravado, but so many of them came home spent, and eerily old.

As the war progressed, our small town shifted incrementally, like a ship that slowly starts to tilt with an uneven load. First, we knew one boy who left. Then we knew another. Soon, Mom was writing notes to other mothers every week, it seemed, filling them with words of encouragement or sympathy in her careful backhand script. I was in the middle phase of a child's life—too young to know everything, too old to know nothing at all. I would be sitting in school with twenty other fifth-graders, and suddenly a classmate would be called into the hall. The assumption was always that another family had gotten bad news from the war.

One time it was our family, but after a really bad scare, the news was good. My cousin Norman was in Vietnam, and for some reason, Mom knew there was a chance that he had been shot. I still remember the call that came two days later. I was sitting on the sofa when the phone rang and my mother rushed to answer. She listened for a few moments, and started to cry. "He's alive!" she yelled. "He's alive." She later said his air mattress had been shot out from under him. I pictured him lying on one of those colorful rafts swimmers used on Lake Erie, and thought Vietnam must be one crazy place.

More than 2 million Americans served in Vietnam. Ohio lost 3,094 of them. The rest of our boys came home, but the ship never righted. Guys I'd known my entire life weren't fun, or funny anymore. No more teasing, no big brother reprimands to get out of the street and quit picking on the little ones. Sometimes I'd look at my friends' older brothers sitting on their front porches and their stares would scare me. I'd look in their eyes and get goose bumps. It was as if they thought I was trying to start a fight just by smiling at them. I'd scamper off, full of questions my father warned me never to ask.

By 1978, I was a college junior and a journalism major on the same college campus where Ohio National Guardsmen had opened fire at an antiwar protest in 1970, killing four students and wounding nine others. I spent most of my days at the student newspaper, *The Daily Kent Stater*, where a wall of windows overlooked Blanket Hill. Until I went to college, I thought everyone knew at least one person who'd fought in Vietnam. About six weeks into my freshman year, I stopped asking.

All this may explain why I was eager on that day in 1978 to read Herr's ferocious account of his year in Vietnam, where he went (in le Carré's phrase) "to the limit in order to make himself a part of the monstrosity he visited." But I was scared too. Not because I was a girl and we didn't "do war." No, I wanted to understand what had happened to the boys in my hometown, and why my childhood seemed so different from that of the kids who grew up in neighborhoods full of college deferments. Six pages in, I knew Herr had answers that would likely mess with my head for a long, long time.

* * *

It's almost hard to remember the parched terrain of literature and movies about the Vietnam War when *Dispatches* was released in 1977. David Halberstam's 1969 book, *The Best and the Brightest*, was a widely respected critique of the war, but he focused on the political and military decision makers who led us into the quagmire. The only well-known movie about Vietnam was John Wayne's *The Green Berets*, an anticommunist screed made in 1968, in large part because Wayne wanted to beef up lagging support for the war. Writing in the *Chicago Sun-Times*, Roger Ebert denounced the film as "propaganda":

> [It] simply will not do as a film about the war in Vietnam. It is offensive not only to those who oppose American policy but even to those who support it. At this moment in our history, locked in the longest and one of the most controversial wars we have ever fought, what we certainly do not need is a movie depicting Vietnam in terms of cowboys and Indians. That is cruel and dishonest and unworthy of the thousands who have died there.

A string of compelling movies would come out a decade after Wayne's, including *Coming Home* (1978) and *Apocalypse Now* (1979), which Herr helped write. (In 1987, he would also contribute to the script of *Full Metal Jacket*.) But as far as popular culture goes, Vietnam was still, if not a blank canvas, a painting without form the year that *Dispatches* hit the shelves.

Critics immediately hailed it as the story of the real Vietnam War, the one told from the view of the grunts on the ground, rather than politicians or military commanders thousands of miles away. Hunter S. Thompson said that Herr "puts all the rest of us in the shade." John Leonard praised it in an idiom closer to the author's: "It is as if Dante had gone to hell with a cassette recording of Jimi Hendrix and a pocketful of pills: our first rock-and-roll war, stoned murder."

Herr, who never trained as a journalist, originally went to Vietnam for *Esquire*, but wrote only one story for the magazine during the time he was there. In his book, he vacillates between scared-out-of-his-bones humility and the occasional, arrogant conviction that, unlike some of the pretty-boy journalists, he was there for the right reasons.

"I could skip the daily briefings," he recalls. Then he continues: "I honestly wanted to know what the form was for those interviews, but some of the reporters I'd ask would get very officious, saying something about

'Command postures,' and look at me as if I was insane. It was probably the kind of look that I gave one of them when he asked me once what I found to talk about with the grunts all the time, expecting me to confide (I think) that I found them as boring as he did."

Other times, Herr sounds far less confident.

"There wasn't a day when someone didn't ask me what I was doing there," he writes. What got him to Vietnam in the first place, he insists, was "the crude but serious belief that you had to be able to look at anything, serious because I acted on it and went, crude because I didn't know, it took the war to teach it, that you were responsible for everything you saw as you were for everything you did."

It took about six years for Herr to write his book. He was candid about the reasons why in a 1992 interview with Eric James Schroeder in *Vietnam, We've All Been There: Interviews with American Writers*. (Schroeder lifted the first part of his title from the last line in *Dispatches*.)

"I was pretty crazy when I came back," he told Schroeder. "For a long time I was, in fact, very crazy. Sometimes I was crazy in a very public way, and after I crashed I was crazy in a very private way. . . . I always believed that there was another door on the other side of me that I could go through and come out of with a book under my arm."

He wrote the first and last chapters, then filled in the middle. It was not, he said, a book about the war. "If somebody were to ask me what it was about, I would say that the secret subject of *Dispatches* was not Vietnam, but that it was a book about writing a book," Herr confessed. "I think that all good books are about writing."

Three years after *Dispatches* was published, Herr moved to London, where he lived for more than a decade. His initial success seemed to have taken a toll on the author. When Paul Ciotti interviewed him for the *Los Angeles Times* in 1990, he described "one of the strangest careers of a contemporary American writer. [Herr] refused to grant interviews. He gave up his once-compulsive world travels and became a dedicated homebody and family man, trading drugs for Gauloises and acid rock for Mozart. He let his leisurely output slow to such a glacial pace that it looked as though he had fallen off the literary radar screen. . . ."

Herr didn't go completely silent. He wrote two more books: a novel about Walter Winchell in 1990, and a 15,000-word essay about Stanley Kubrick that morphed into a slim biography in 2000. But neither won even a fraction of the praise and attention that had been heaped on his debut.

There are many quotable nuggets from *Dispatches*. "Conventional journalism could no more reveal this war than conventional firepower could win it," is an oft-quoted favorite. "There's nothing so embarrassing as when things go wrong in a war," is another. These one-liners are clever. They're quoted because they're short and snappy, but they don't reflect why *Dispatches* changed the way we talked about Vietnam. For a better sense of the book's impact, consider this passage on the many ways a man could die:

> You could die in a sudden bloodburning crunch as your chopper hit the ground like dead weight, you could fly apart so that your pieces would never be gathered, you could take one neat round in the lung and go out hearing only the bubble of the last few breaths, you could die in the last stage of malaria with that faint tapping in your ears, and that could happen to you after months of firefights and rockets and machine guns. Enough, too many, were saved for that, and you always hoped that no irony would attend your passing. You could end in a pit somewhere with a spike through you, everything stopped forever except for the one or two motions, purely involuntary, as though you could kick it all away and come back. You could fall down dead so that the medics would have to spend half an hour looking for the hole that killed you, getting more and more spooked as the search went on. You could be shot, mined, grenaded, rocketed, mortared, sniped at, blown up and away so that your leavings had to be dropped into a sagging poncho and carried to Graves Registration, that's all she wrote. It was almost marvelous.

Herr's book was as unfiltered as a private journal, and as honest as a man on his deathbed. Sometimes he wrote in cool and measured prose, like a hip historian. Most of the time, he raced across the page like the men he described as "talking in short violent bursts as though they were afraid they might not get to finish." Perhaps he was always like that; more likely, he eventually absorbed the grunts' cadences as his own. Thirty years after reading the book for the first time, I still have the same gut response: at least I understand why I will never understand what happened to our boys in Vietnam. That may sound like small consolation to those who don't remember the war, but the realization that some horrors are beyond my comprehension liberated me from a guilt I couldn't name at twenty-one, and still struggle with now.

Back in 1978, I read Herr's book in one sleepless night. I thought about it for a couple of days, read it again. Then I mailed my copy of *Dispatches* to my parents with a note pleading that they read it. Weeks passed, and I finally called. My mother said she couldn't read it because it was making her cry too much. Dad wouldn't even pick it up. To him, *Dispatches* was 260 pages of reasons why they'd sent me away to college. If we learned anything in our blue-collar town, in our factory worker's family, it was that college kids were special, they were protected, they got away with things. Like war, for example.

Nearly 80 percent of those who fought in Vietnam came from rural and blue-collar families. My mother and father would end up dying in their sixties after working hard to make sure they changed the odds for their four kids. In 1978, I was only the first to go to college. Dad, who often worked double shifts at a power plant on Lake Erie, had no time to look back, and no interest in Michael Herr's version of America.

I said earlier that I had to find my courage to read *Dispatches* back then. As it turned out, I needed to find a different kind of courage to reread it in 2010. I knew to brace for its relentless loop of gore and terror, but I didn't remember many of the specifics, and this time they clawed at my heart, and my conscience. Fatally wounded boys cry for their mothers. A man wraps his wife's oatmeal cookie in foil, plastic and three pairs of socks to keep it safe for months in the jungle.

And sometimes, numbers speak horrible truths. The National Archives rank Vietnam casualties by age. Of the dead, 9,705 were twenty-one; 14,095 were twenty; and 8,283 were nineteen.

Twelve of them were only seventeen.

I am no longer a young college student struggling to imagine such things. I am a middle-aged wife and mother who knows life is unspeakably better when all of your children have already lived longer than the majority of the men who died in Vietnam. I am the grandmother of a two-year-old boy, born in a country fighting two wars with no end in sight.

* * *

There's a footnote to Michael Herr's story, and it's a big one. As a journalist, I was taken aback to discover that, while *Dispatches* was published as nonfiction, Herr always thought of it as a novel. "I don't think that it's any secret that there is talk in the book that's invented," he told Schroeder.

"But it is invented out of that voice that I heard so often and that made such penetration into my head. . . . I don't really want to go into that no-man's-land about what really happened and what didn't really happen and where you draw the line. Everything in *Dispatches* happened *for* me, even if it didn't necessarily happen *to* me." Later, he adds:

> There are errors of fact in the book. I'm not happy about this. When the Khe Sahn piece was published [as an essay before the book], I had a really beautiful letter from a colonel who had been stationed there; he corrected me on various points of fact. I lost the letter, and it didn't turn up again until after the book was in print. . . . I couldn't bear to go in and make the revisions myself. I was tapped out. I was exhausted from the project. Including the year in the war, I had spent eight years working on it, and I just couldn't do any more.

It's doubtful that Herr could have pulled this off in our current climate of online fact-checkers and self-anointed "citizen journalists." It is too easy to imagine Sergeant So-and-So from Cleveland, Mississippi, yelling on FOX News, "I was on the Langvei attack, and Mr. Herr is lying!" Or an anonymous blogger posting "Top Ten Reasons Michael Herr Is a Traitor," followed by 413 comments, 390 of them irrelevant to the post at hand.

I wonder if the critics would have been harsher to Herr had they known of his errors and inventions before writing their reviews. Even if we read it as fiction, *Dispatches* is a work of enormous power, but would its sense of urgency and loss be diminished?

Not for me. I have never had the guts to cover a war, and doubt I could ever risk my safety, and my sanity, as Herr did when he was in Vietnam. I have neither the right nor the will to pass judgment on how he brought home the war to millions of Americans who had yet to face it. And ultimately, whatever its flaws may be as straight journalism, his book is a tribute to the young men he met in Vietnam. In the 2001 documentary, *First Kill*, it's clear that Herr was unable to forget them: "It's their voices. It's their amazing eloquence. My book is full of them. You know, that's really what my book is. These guys were semi-demi-literate kids from a really unfavorable social background, who just had such a dignity. I couldn't help but find that really moving, and really persuasive."

Michael Herr was changed by what he saw, and what he endured. I am grateful that he lived to tell the tale, that he survived to write simple descriptions like this one: "He was the kind of kid that would go into the high-school gym alone and shoot baskets for the half-hour before the basketball team took it over for practice, not good enough yet for the team but determined."

Sounds like half the boys I knew.

Until they went to Vietnam.

Michael Shapiro

CORNELIUS RYAN'S
THE LONGEST DAY

In 1957, an expatriate Irish newspaperman struggling to make a buck after
his most recent employer went under began making the rounds of magazine editors and book publishers, hoping to get someone to help foot the
bill for a hazily formed idea about a fifteenth-anniversary retelling of the
events of June 6, 1944: D-Day. Here was the true, humble, and all-but-
forgotten beginning to the modern age of Journalism as Literature.

Over the years the trade had produced occasional flashes of inspiration
in which a writer—Daniel Defoe, Rebecca West, Joseph Mitchell, W. C.
Heinz, John Hersey—took a turn at bringing to a true story the qualities
of fiction. But those moments came, and always went, and did not much
alter the journalistic landscape. That began to change in 1957, when Cornelius Ryan, staked by the least hip of all magazines, *Reader's Digest*, began
placing ads in newspapers and trade publications, searching for men and
women who had been in Normandy that day. From those ads sprung a
great journalistic enterprise that would culminate, two years later, with the
publication of *The Longest Day*.

The book was a triumph, earning rave reviews and sales that, within
a few years, would stretch into the tens of millions in eighteen different
languages. And yet, in latter-day journalistic circles, *The Longest Day* is an
afterthought—a book recalled not for spawning a revolution but for its

big-screen adaptation of the same name, which seems to appear on cable early every June.

Conventional wisdom has it that the uprising that continues to define how so much journalism reads, and how so many journalists prefer to think of themselves, began, like so much else that feels transformative about American culture, in the 1960s. It was then that such icons as Tom Wolfe, Gay Talese, Joan Didion, and Hunter S. Thompson began producing so much terrific work that by 1972, Wolfe would look back and proclaim that a "new journalism" had been born. Wolfe took it a step further. He argued that New Journalism—now a decade into its full-blown adolescence—was not only trampling on the flower gardens of the craft's more sober practices but also stomping upon the topiary gem of American letters: the Big Novel.

Wolfe's essays in *New York* Magazine were followed a year later by the publication of the Scouts Handbook for young journalists, his coedited *New Journalism* anthology. By then, legions of eager reporters had shoved aside the he-said-she-said-can-you-spell-it-for-me ways of the past and embraced the idea that they could bring to their work the sensibilities and techniques of fiction. Novelists too had taken up the call, abandoning the garret and loading up on #2 pencils and steno pads before heading out across the land to see with their own eyes and hear with their own ears. Truman Capote, celebrated as a very hot novelist at twenty-two before finding himself in a creative trough, returned to New York from Holcomb, Kansas, in 1965 proclaiming that with *In Cold Blood*, he had invented an entirely new literary form: the nonfiction novel.

Wolfe had presented a template for the many ways a writer could make a name for himself. And perhaps the combination of that collected work and the pyrotechnics of his prose obscured the larger lesson he preached. Yes, the New Journalism was about attaining in nonfiction the realism that novelists had abandoned, or ignored. But to achieve what Talese and Thompson had accomplished meant performing the very act that Norman Mailer, whose best work was arguably his nonfiction, had dismissed as "chores": reporting.

Wolfe extolled the virtues of immersion, a school of gathering information in which "the basic reporting unit is no longer the datum, the piece of information, but the scene. . . ." To report, he went on, meant hanging out, watching, listening, taking it all in to achieve a novelistic effect. But his enthusiasm for the thrill of the hunt came with a warning, offered in the simplest and most sadly overlooked words in his essay: "Reporting never becomes any easier because you have done it many times."

It was easier, then, to focus on the writing. After all, it was in the writing where you could show how you'd sweated. To be regarded merely as a good reporter was to be dismissed as the sort of person in whom the object of one's desire sees only a friend.

So it is not surprising that within a few years of the publication of that essay and anthology, the revolution that Wolfe had evoked with such delight had ground to a halt. In its place would come the very sort of ossification and hewing to convention (*"What, no anecdotal lede?"*) that Wolfe and his cadre had worked so hard to crack. More and more, journalists would trade in the most expedient forms: stylistic flourishes and one-liners and the witty turn of phrase that is the last redoubt of the fellow who, as Faulkner once said, can write but has nothing to say.

The revolution built upon reporting in service of achieving the feel of fiction was never about the writing, at least not for its own sake. But who cared? So many young journalists, myself included, did not necessarily think of ourselves as reporters.

But Wolfe did. And so did Cornelius Ryan.

* * *

I will confess to a romantic attachment to *The Longest Day* that has nothing to do with journalism. It was the first "grown-up" book I read. I was not a reader, but I had seen the movie and watched *Combat!* on TV and, in my pre-Vietnam growing up, was a sucker for war stories. Having dipped in and out of the Landmark young-adult books on great battles and heroes, I was ready for something more. My father, hoping to find a book that might catch me up, handed me *The Longest Day*. It worked; I read. At least, I read that one.

He did it again, for sentimental reasons, in 1978, giving me a new copy after I had moved to Chicago for a newspaper job. I do not recall rereading the book. I was too much in the throes of Wolfe and company and, given where my aspirations lay, did not see how *The Longest Day* and its author could be of much use.

It would take a long time and a good many stories before I began to fall in love with reporting. The realization came as I began to understand that while my writing would after a time improve only incrementally, reporting was a craft that could, if done ambitiously, remain beyond perfecting. The lonely and maddening business of writing could be fueled not by what dexterity with words I could summon but by all the many things I had to find out. I fell in love with reporting only after I was old enough to appreciate that, journalistically speaking, it could keep me young.

Which is what led me back to *The Longest Day*. I had not opened the book in many years. And yet the story, or rather the many small stories that filled the narrative, had stayed with me. I had seen the movie from time to time over the years. It is a remarkably faithful adaptation—Ryan had worked on the screenplay. But was it the film or my early memories of the book that drew me back? Or was it something else entirely: my growing realization that the qualities that made the book endure—the precise details, the way each of Ryan's many set pieces unfolded so quickly, even as the sentences were packed with multiple facts—could come only through an approach to reporting that I had long considered secondary to the words themselves?

I opened the book on the eve of a long weekend. I was hooked after a single page. Something was taking place in the telling of this story that transcended the journalistic equivalent of mere looks—a richness, a depth. A little like love, not as it happens for teenagers, but for adults.

Ryan opens his story in the coastal village of La Roche-Guyon. He lingers there for only two pages, long enough to establish the date (June 4), the weather (gray, misty), and the sounds of dawn (a church bell ending the nighttime curfew and heralding day 1,451 of the German occupation) before introducing his most compelling character, Field Marshal Erwin Rommel. When we meet him, the German commander—and D-Day's biggest loser—is awaiting the invasion in the village's castle. It is a neatly accomplished piece of foreshadowing; Ryan sprinkles in his facts without gumming up the machinery, and delivers an implicit promise to the reader. *You want details? You want characters? I've got a million of 'em.*

The author immediately makes good, tightening his focus on Hitler's most celebrated general:

> In the ground-floor room he used as an office, Rommel was alone.
> He sat behind a massive Renaissance desk, working by the light
> of a single desk lamp. The room was large and high-ceilinged.

Along one wall stretched a faded Gobelin tapestry. On another the haughty face of Duke François de la Rochefoucauld—a seventeenth-century writer of maxims and an ancestor of the present Duke—looked down out of a heavy gold frame. There were a few chairs casually placed on the highly polished parquet floor and thick draperies at the windows, but little else.

Nothing slows the eye's journey across the page; the author feels no compulsion to call out, "Look over here, it's me!" And this makes it easy to miss what is so striking about this otherwise simple passage: the efficient accumulation of fact.

We learn that Rommel was a) alone, b) seated at a desk that was c) massive and d) Renaissance and fitted with a single lamp, and that he worked under the gaze of e) Duke François de la Rochefoucauld, whose face was f) haughty and whose portrait was framed in g) gold. And then, quite subtly, Ryan offers a quick peek at his character: "In particular, there was nothing of Rommel in this room but himself." Not a photograph of his wife (Lucie-Maria) or son (Manfred, age fifteen) or mementos of his great victories in North Africa, such as the field marshal's baton Hitler had presented him (eighteen inches, three pounds, gold, red velvet covered with gold eagles and black swastikas) because such extravagance, Ryan writes, was alien to Rommel, a man who "cared so little for food that he sometimes forgot to eat."

Rommel did not know when the Allies were coming nor where they would land. But, Ryan tells us, his defenses were stretched thin and he decided to return to Germany and plead for more materiel from Hitler. He would stop at home along the way to present a pair of shoes (gray suede, size five and a half) to his wife on her birthday, June 6.

Size five and a half? How did he get that?

* * *

Cornelius Ryan was at Normandy twice on D-Day, the first time on a bomber flying over the beaches, the second time on a patrol boat that took him back after he landed in England. He had turned twenty-four the day before. He had been working as a war correspondent for London's *The Daily Telegraph* since 1943, having come to London from Dublin in 1940, and to journalism a year later at Reuters, after attending a school where he studied violin. He covered the air war over Germany—perilous work—as well as Patton's Third Army, then reported from the Pacific.

In 1947, Ryan moved to the United States, where he became a naturalized citizen and, eventually, a writer for *Time*, *Newsweek*, and, until its demise in 1956, *Collier's*. By then, he had written four books, including two about Douglas MacArthur and another, *One Minute to Ditch*, about an airliner's ocean landing. He also published a good many magazine stories that, taken together, reflected less a budding literary career—"I Rode in the World's Fastest Sub"—than the workmanlike yield of a man who knew how to churn out copy.

But one story did suggest that, given the chance to pursue the best material, Ryan could produce memorable work. In 1956, the liner *Andrea Doria* collided with a Swedish ship off the coast of Nantucket and sank. Ryan set about reconstructing the collision, the rescue of all but 46 of the ship's 1,706 passengers, and most memorably, the drama of a husband and wife who had switched beds the night before, only to be woken when a beam split their cabin—separating them, as it turns out, forever. The writing was at times overdone. But the reporting, which included the surviving husband's moment-by-moment account of his wife's demise, was a harbinger of the big projects to come.

Ryan had initially proposed a D-Day book about only the first two or three hours of the invasion. But then he began to report, and his ads ("Personal: Were You There on 6 June 1944?") yielded thousands of responses. He followed up with a three-page questionnaire that could serve as a primer for reconstructing a narrative: Where did you land and at what time? What was the trip like during the crossing? Do you remember, for example, any conversations you had or how you passed the time? Were you wounded? Do you remember what it was like—that is, do you remember whether you felt any pain or were you so surprised that you felt nothing?

One thousand one hundred and fifty people wrote back. And of that group, he interviewed, alone or with his assistants, 172. Ryan's daughter, Victoria Bida, told me that her father had once been away for 18 months reporting, suggesting that to find the man, the reporter, you need look no farther than his files. And to read the files—to deconstruct how the book was assembled, to connect names and stories in the book with questionnaires, interviews, letters, diaries, and regimental histories—is to feel yourself in the presence, so many years later, of a man compelled to learn *everything*.

Here, for instance, was the questionnaire from Lieutenant Donald Anderson of the 29th Infantry Division, who wrote about getting shot: "No pain, just stunned. Figured my brains were spilled all over my helmet." Here was Ryan's interview with General Maxwell Taylor, who commanded the 101st Airborne Division and who told him what it had been like parachuting into a dark field: "Lonesome as hell." And here was the interview with Private Aloysius Damski, a Pole who had been forced to join the German 716th Infantry Division, who told of playing a card game called "scat" on the night before the invasion, then peeling away from his unit so that he could surrender to the British.

Then there was the material on Rommel, who committed suicide in October 1944 after he was implicated in a plot to murder Hitler. Ryan had the general's diaries (nary an entry without comment about his dog) and an interview with his widow and son. But it was his adjutant, Captain Hellmuth Lang, who proved to be an interviewer's dream. Lang recalled all the many telling details of the morning before the invasion, when Rommel, after a breakfast of tea and a slice of white bread with butter and honey, set out at precisely 6:47 a.m. in a black convertible Horch for his home in Herrlingen, where he would celebrate his wife's birthday before continuing on for his meeting with Hitler. Frau Rommel later produced the birthday-gift shoes, long since resoled. And Lang, bless him, recalled the size: five and a half.

But Ryan was not only hunting for the small bits. As it happened, the Germans wanted it known that Rommel was not with his troops on D-Day because he was with the Führer. Not so, Lang told him. He was at home—a discovery that was as thrilling as it was frustrating. Now he would have to rewrite the first chapter, and was already feeling overwhelmed by the task of culling, cataloguing, and deciding how best to use all the material he was gathering. "I do not know how I'm going to do this right now," he wrote his wife, Kathryn, a novelist who had also been his most valued aide.

And then, after he was done, he began doing the same thing all over again. Two more books followed: *The Last Battle* (1966), in which he recounted the fall of Berlin, and *A Bridge Too Far* (1974), the story of the Allies' botched attempt to bring the war to a quick end in 1944. The latter is his most poignant and, at times, angry book; the first two, after all, ended in triumph. Like its predecessors, *A Bridge Too Far* tells of the personal courage of so many foot soldiers. But it also recounts the hubris of the commanders who sent those men into battle, an agonizing story of needless carnage that Ryan raced to finish as he was dying.

He had been diagnosed with prostate cancer at fifty, and despite a grim prognosis, had endured the rigors of his treatment and outlived by three years his doctors' grave predictions. But by the spring of 1973, with *A Bridge Too Far* still not done, he wrote to an old friend, the San Francisco columnist Herb Caen, about the burdens of what had been his secret illness, and about the career he had crafted.

"I am three years late with it and the publishers are screaming," he wrote. "The advances have been spent and we are trying to keep our heads above water with the hope that the book will be finished within the next four to six weeks."

He had sold, he believed, between 25 and 35 million copies of *The Longest Day* and 400,000 hardcover copies of *The Last Battle* in the United States alone. Yet each book had cost him some $150,000 to research. "I have no less than 7,000 books on every aspect of World War II. My files contain some 16,000 different interviews with Germans, British, French, etc.," he wrote. "Then there is the chronology of each battle, 5x7 cards, detailing each movement by hour for the particular work I'm engaged in. You may think this is all a kind of madness, an obsession. I suppose it is."

The books brought him fame and, even after deducting his research expenses, wealth. But as he confessed to Caen, he wished they'd also brought him a measure of professional recognition. "I've never seen myself as a writer but only as a journalist," he wrote. Still, he hoped that his last book might bring him a Pulitzer. The Pulitzer board had not yet established a category for general nonfiction, and Ryan understood that he would find it hard to compete with academics for the big prize.

"So there's probably little chance that I may be cited for a Pulitzer because so many of these bastards sit on the board," he wrote, "but it would be nice to get one anyway." (For the record, the 1975 prize in history went to *Jefferson and His Time, Volumes 1–5*, by Dumas Malone.)

Ryan was fifty-four when he died in November 1974, survived by his wife, son, and daughter. The material he had gathered in twenty years of reporting about the war went to Ohio University in Athens, where the dean of the College of Communications was an old friend. The collection's curator, Doug McCabe, told me that even now, sixty-six years after D-Day, historians from around the world, as well as the children and grandchildren of men who fought that day, stop by to search through Ryan's papers in the archive center of the library. It is, he said, the most heavily used collection in the center.

Meanwhile, *The Longest Day* was reissued in 1994 for the fiftieth anniversary of D-Day. It still sells—a fact that belies the glaring omission of Ryan's work from so many anthologies of literary journalism, and also offers a powerful lesson for a trade trying to figure out what people will pay to read. There is nothing, it turns out, like a densely reported story propelled by the palpable sense of a reporter chasing *his* story.

In a sense, Cornelius Ryan started reporting *The Longest Day* on June 6, 1944, and never really stopped. That day, that war, was his story. And when a reporter comes back with something that, as Norman Maclean once wrote, "tells him something about himself," readers know it. They feel it on the page and in the prose, and willingly join in that relentless need to know, and to make sense of things.

Ryan, it turns out, did learn something of himself in his work, and came to know himself well enough to have it inscribed on his tombstone, beneath his name and the years of his too-short life. A single word: "Reporter."

Douglas McCollam

—

JOHN MCPHEE'S
ANNALS OF THE FORMER WORLD

I first encountered the writer John McPhee about ten years ago on a remote stretch of the Salmon River in the wilds of northern Alaska just inside the Arctic Circle. That's where *he* was, at least. I was sitting in the sun
outside a small restaurant near my office in midtown Manhattan. But such
was McPhee's evocation of the Kobuk Valley landscape that it was easy
to look at the flow of traffic up Third Avenue and overlay the taxis, buses,
and buildings with darting graylings, marauding grizzlies, and stands of
virgin willow trees.

I was a latecomer to the tribe of McPhee readers. For some reason,
despite avidly consuming the work of other in-house masters at *The New
Yorker* such as Joseph Mitchell and A. J. Liebling, I'd managed to avoid
McPhee. I'd nod sagely when his name came up in conversation, but I
never actually sat down to read his stuff. I vaguely associated him with the
New Journalism of the 1960s, but where I'd been drawn to gawp at the
stylistic pyrotechnics of Tom Wolfe, Hunter S. Thompson, and Truman
Capote, I viewed McPhee, with his forensic dissections of flora and fauna
as, well, a trifle dull. Twenty thousand words on the virtues of Florida
oranges or Bill Bradley's jump shot? No thanks.

That changed right about the time I decided to leave my legal career
and become a writer, or at least a journalist. My first job was editing a

three-hole-punch financial monthly then put out by Steve Brill's *American Lawyer*. The job came with a small office, two dutiful junior editors, and David Marcus, a hyperkinetic staff writer who, with scant prompting, would hold forth at length and with surprising candor on the failings of his editors (myself included), the virtues of Princeton lacrosse, and the writing of John McPhee. Hero worship is too uncritical a quality to manifest in a character as irascible as Marcus, but his enthusiasm for McPhee was ardent and infectious. More than once I gingerly approached Marcus's desk to investigate the fate of some overdue article on, say, the takeover of a Connecticut car-parts company, only to find him manically sifting through a mound of index cards, because "that's how McPhee" organized his research (though I felt pretty sure there was more actual organization in McPhee's system). Usually when I attempted some judicious pruning of a Marcus magnum opus, he'd speed-walk into my office and begin denouncing me as a ham-handed simpleton. "Read McPhee," he'd often admonish, with a mixture of pity and irritation. Only then, it seemed, might I hope to grasp the Marcusian literary vision.

As there appeared to be little likelihood of avoiding such encounters with Marcus, in the spring of 1998 I decided to take his advice and picked up a copy of McPhee's *Coming Into the Country*, already known to many (but not to me) as a nonfiction classic. Published in 1977, the book recounts McPhee's journeys in the Alaskan backcountry. Though I dedicated big chunks of hours to reading the book, it nevertheless took me a while to get through it, as I'd often stop and reread several pages trying to figure out what McPhee was up to. I particularly rehashed the book's front section, "The Encircled River," in which McPhee, like a Victorian illusionist, somehow manages to finish the story at the exact time and place on the river where it began. The time shift in the narrative is so subtle that I drifted right through it, arriving at the end point blinking like a sleepy child awoken from the backseat of a car already parked in the driveway. For an apprentice nonfiction writer, it was a revelation.

* * *

Thus inducted into the clan of McPhee admirers, I was primed for the publication later that year of *Annals of the Former World*. The book is a compilation of writing on geology McPhee began in 1978 when he published a short item about a road cut on Interstate 80 west of New York

City. Over the following twenty years, that initial story led McPhee to make a series of trips across America in the company of geologists, through whom he would explore both the geologic history of a region and the history of geology itself. Those travels resulted in four separate books: *Basin and Range*, *In Suspect Terrain*, *Rising from the Plains*, and *Assembling California*. For the publication of *Annals*, these were joined by a fifth and final section, *Crossing the Craton*.

Even for a writer known for pulping juice out of seemingly desiccated subject matter, publishing a 660-page doorstop on geology seemed a bit extreme. There is always with McPhee a gnawing sense that perhaps he is choosing his subjects precisely for their apparent dullness, tossing down the gauntlet, as it were, before contemporary sensibilities of what makes for good stories. In a time when so many nonfiction writers work with one eye trained on Hollywood, hoping to follow their narrative arcs and high concepts into the sunlit uplands of first dollar gross, McPhee's work remains resolutely uncinematic.

That is certainly the case with *Annals*, whose frequent declivities, buried geosynclines, and discordant batholiths make it too-rugged terrain for Hollywood to file a claim on. Which is not the same thing as saying the subject is bland. Indeed, as McPhee notes early on in the book, geology is known as a descriptive science. And so it is. In making the road cuts yield up their secrets, McPhee finds keys to time machines parked at regular intervals by the side of the highway. Consider McPhee's examination of a canyon wall in Nevada that holds sand and pebbles from the ancient shoreline of the Meramecian straits off the then-coast of North America:

> The strait was warm and equatorial. The equator ran through the present site of San Diego, up through Colorado and Nebraska, and on through the site of Lake Superior. The lake would not be dug for nearly three hundred and forty million years. If in the Meramecian you were to have followed the present route of Interstate 80 moving east, you would have raised the coast of North America near the Wyoming border, and landed on a red beach. Gradually you would have ascended through equatorial fern forests, in red soil, to a high point somewhere near Laramie, to begin there a long general downgrade among low hills to Grand Island, Nebraska, where you would have come to an arm of the sea. The far shore was

104

Douglas McCollam

four hundred miles to the east, where the Mississippi River is now, and beyond it was a low, wet, humid, flat terrain, dense with ferns and fern trees—Illinois, Indiana, Ohio. Halfway across Ohio, you would have come to a second epicratonic sea, its far shore in central Pennsylvania. In New Jersey you would have begun to ascend mountains and ever higher mountains, their summits girt with ice and capped with snow, not unlike Mt. Kenya. . . . Reaching the site of the George Washington Bridge, you would have been at a considerable altitude, looking at mountains and more mountains before you in future Africa.

I'm tempted to say that passages like this one and many others in *Annals of the Former World* have had a lingering effect on me, but that does not quite describe the impact of the book. Many books haunt, but while I may have pondered the cruel fate of Tolstoy's Madame Karenina or felt the visceral despair of Saint Augustine even after returning their stories to the shelf, no work has altered my perception of the world and our place in it more than McPhee's geology tome. It caused a shift in conscience, an alteration in the currents of my thought that, even now, carve out fresh new channels for my perceptions to tumble down.

Usually those kinds of seismic events are produced between the covers of religious or philosophical tracts or, perhaps, by a great novel. But geology? Over the years I've often attempted to explain the book's tug on my psyche, but usually only receive looks of bemused indulgence. Such reactions have often made me wonder if *Annals*, like *Finnegans Wake*, is one of those books that many have on the shelf but few have actually read. I raised the question with David Remnick, McPhee's editor at *The New Yorker*, of whether the book, despite having won a Pulitzer Prize, is sometimes overlooked by readers. "I think it really is an underrated masterpiece," said Remnick, a former student of McPhee's at Princeton. "It got made fun of a little bit as 'that story about rocks.'"

Trying to explain the book's power, I've clumsily equated its effect to a kind of personal Copernican revolution, one that stripped away lingering notions of childhood religion and permanently colored my perception of human history. The endorsement of Copernicus's heliocentric view of the universe in the early seventeenth century, you might recall, caused Galileo to be placed under house arrest for life by the Vatican. After reading *An-*

nals, I better understood how unsettling a bit of heresy was Copernican astronomy, because it, like the book, moves mankind far, far, far from the center of the narrative of creation and existence.

To illustrate how humankind stands in relation to the larger sweep of events, McPhee supplies the useful notion of "animal time." As creatures of animal time, human beings tend to walk around in a bubble of five generations: two back; two forward. Occasionally, we may stretch a rung or two beyond this construct, but generally speaking that's our comfort zone. To help contrast animal time with geologic time, McPhee notes that geologists sometimes use a calendar year to represent the history of the earth. In the first ten months, the Precambrian period, the basement of time, there is little in the way of fossil records:

> Dinosaurs appear in the middle of December and are gone the day after Christmas. The last ice sheet melts on December 31st at one minute before midnight, and the Roman Empire lasts five seconds.

McPhee then offers a try-at-home exercise to help break the bonds of animal time:

> With your arms spread wide again to represent all the time on earth, look at one hand with its line of life. The Cambrian begins in the wrist, and the Permian Extinction is at the outer end of the palm. All of the Cenozoic is in a fingerprint, and in a single stroke with a medium-grained nail file you could eradicate human history.

For geologists, then, the human condition appears quite different:

> They often liken humanity's presence on earth to a brief visitation from elsewhere in space, its luminous, explosive characteristics consisting not merely of the burst of population in the twentieth century, but of the whole residence of people on earth—a single detonation, resembling nothing so much as a nuclear implosion with its successive neutron generations, whole generations following one another once every hundred-millionth of a second. . . . The human mind may not have evolved enough to be able to comprehend deep time. It may only be able to measure it. . . . Primordial inhibition may stand in the way. On the geologic time scale, a human lifetime is reduced to a brevity that is too inhibiting to think about. The mind blocks the information.

Obviously, the effect of letting this notion of deep time seep into one's conscience is not always comforting—or productive. When I came home to New Orleans after Hurricane Katrina I heard many fellow Orleanians talk about the traditions and history of the city that had to be saved. I found myself thinking that the surrounding ground was lying to us. With its 500-year-old oak trees draped in Spanish moss and its eighteenth-century historic landmarks, the landscape of New Orleans does appear old—from the perspective of animal time almost primordial. In geologic time, though, it's quite young and unstable. The Mississippi River deposited the ground on which the city is built only in the last 10,000 years—a minute ago in geologic time—and will take it back just as fast. On the other hand, escaping from animal time can be comforting as well. Whenever ethnic violence flares up at home or abroad, I take some solace in the fact that just 50,000 years ago we were all one small tribe living in Africa. Surely, then, we can come to recognize our own family whom we left only a moment ago.

* * *

The achievement of McPhee in writing *Annals* isn't to teach you to measure time, which is an intellectual enterprise, but to make you feel it, to guide your senses in peering around the built-in barriers that retard our detection of its true dimensions. He does this in a manner befitting his subject matter: through mass and constant pressure. When we talked, David Remnick told me that, although he had read all the sections of the book when they were first published, they somehow gained power when collected together, accumulated and compressed, as it were, to a far greater density.

It's the kind of density that has its detractors. McPhee is revered by many writers, particularly those "McPhinos" (like Remnick) who took his writing course, The Literature of Fact, at Princeton. Yet there are others who find his work ponderous, his choice of subjects off-putting, and his exalted status among egghead journalists irritating. In 2005, Michael Wolff, who covers the media for *Vanity Fair* magazine, took a swipe at "the cult of John McPhee," calling the man himself "a writer of fabled factuality and unstylishness, who, I would wager, has seldom been read to the end by anybody other than his acolytes."

I guess that means I should be fitted for vestments, because I find it hard to see how anyone who has started a McPhee story could put it down, a fact of which I was reminded not long after agreeing to write this assessment of *Annals*. Looking for my copy, I realized that I had left it at my apartment in Washington, D.C., so I went by a local bookstore in New Orleans to see if they had it in stock. No luck, but they did have *Coming Into the Country*, the book that had first sparked my affinity for McPhee. It was a beautiful day, and I sat outside on the lawn of an old mansion that's been converted to a small library in my neighborhood, a place where I sometimes go to write. For a while I tried to read with a critical eye, plumbing the text for clues as to what so rankles McPhee's critics (the penchant for Melvillean lists? the sometimes glacial pacing?) and also for what I liked (Melvillean lists, glacial pacing). I was dutiful for a while, but the sun was warm and as the afternoon wore on I ended up putting my pen aside and lying back on the grass. On the avenue in front of the library, the after-school traffic swelled and knotted, but it was too late by then to disturb my reverie. I had already slipped back onto the Salmon River, and all the honking SUVs were snarling grizzly bears.

Scott Sherman

/

MARSHALL FRADY'S
WALLACE

A few months before he died in a car accident, David Halberstam published a droll, melancholy homage to his colleague and friend Marshall Frady, who lost a prolonged battle with cancer in 2004. (The essay appeared as a new introduction to two books by Frady that his publisher reissued in 2006, *Billy Graham: A Parable of American Righteousness* and *Jesse: The Life and Pilgrimage of Jesse Jackson*.) Halberstam described a luminous interlude in his career, from 1967 to 1971, when both he and Frady were staff writers at *Harper's* under the celebrated editorship of Willie Morris, who transformed a stodgy magazine into an exhilarating one that printed works by Norman Mailer, William Styron, Gay Talese, and others.

When he took over *Harper's* in 1967, Morris was already acquainted with Frady's work for *Newsweek* and *The Saturday Evening Post*. Morris considered Frady "a genius of the language" and hired him when he was twenty-eight. The two men, Southern boys transplanted to the glittering literary salons of Manhattan, had an affectionate bond: Frady called Morris "Sire" and sometimes "Boss." But Morris was manning the helm of a foundering vessel: *Harper's* bled $150,000 a year, and in 1971 Morris was forced out by the ruling Cowles family. "It all boiled down to the money men and the literary men," he lamented in his resignation letter. "And, as always, the money men won."

Morris's departure jolted the literary world. Mailer, Styron, Talese, Bill Moyers, and Tom Wicker declared that they would boycott *Harper's* as long as the Cowles family owned it, and the four staff writers hired by Morris—Frady among them—resigned in solidarity with him. Toward the end of Halberstam's essay, we see Frady lurching through the 1970s, writing for magazines, and, in search of financial stability, eventually settling into a career in television, joining ABC News in 1979. "It was not where he should have been," Halberstam noted, although "fortunately, he kept writing books even as television seduced him and he in turn seduced television."

The books themselves remain seductive, and Halberstam's final assessment of Frady offers an unequivocal explanation of their allure:

> What is remarkable about his body of work is how well it stands up, that it is curiously timeless—as so much of the journalism of that era is not—that it comes together finally not as fragments but as a whole, a universe of George Wallace, Billy Graham, Jesse Jackson, Martin Luther King Jr., and all the contemporary Snopeses and other tricksters and dime-store rascals who populate his book *Southerners: A Journalist's Odyssey* (1980), as if all of it put together forms a kind of autobiography.

"I grew up not only a Southern Baptist, but a Southern Baptist minister's son," Frady wrote in *Southerners*, "in the small cities and towns of my father's nomadic pastorates over the inland South." Part of Frady's early youth was spent in Augusta, Georgia, inside his father's church. What he recalled more than anything else was "the sensation of being recurrently pent there for long static ruthlessly abstracted hours of piety and propriety and the commemoration of a wholly inscrutable theology."

He inevitably warmed to the sensations of the wider world: at age twelve he found a stray copy of *The New Yorker* ("it was like a secret pulsation from another cosmos"), after which he came across John Steinbeck's *East of Eden*, and then Shakespeare, Dickens, Sinclair Lewis, and H. L. Mencken. Frady would soon discover his principal literary influence, William Faulkner, "an experience," he wrote, "that a lot of Southern boys spend the rest of their lives trying to recover from."

In 1965, Joe Cumming, the Atlanta bureau chief of *Newsweek*, heard about a gifted twenty-five-year-old reporter who was toiling for the *Au-*

gusta Chronicle and asked him for a writing sample. "The next morning he turned in a seventeen-page piece—I think on himself," Cumming told Halberstam. "All I remember was how good it was." Already, in his mid-twenties, Frady was in full possession of an immensely sophisticated prose style. Readers of *Newsweek* were soon encountering passages like this, from "A Death in Lowndes County," published in 1965: "The trial was held in the fall—pale mornings and dreary afternoons flicked by drizzles, with a small dim sun suspended over drab fields of dried corn stalks: a cool and quiescent weather strangely abstracted from that glowering summer afternoon, the instant astonishing flash and roar and blurting blood of the deed itself." (The deed was the shotgunning of two young civil rights workers by a Hayneville, Alabama, sheriff.)

It was at *Newsweek* in 1966, while covering the Alabama gubernatorial race, that Frady first began to contemplate a book about George Wallace—"a kind of journalistic novel, employing all the stagework, style and larger vision of the novelist." Two years later, *Wallace* was published to wide acclaim, during a period when the "New Journalism" was expanding the boundaries of literary nonfiction.

When I picked up the book in 1996, in a reissued Random House paperback, I knew only the basics about Wallace: that his 1963 inaugural address contained the words "segregation now . . . segregation tomorrow . . . segregation forever"; that he ran four insurgent campaigns for president, in which he galvanized white, blue-collar voters with a stark, earthy rhetoric that invoked a nation overrun by hippies, homosexuals, feminists, black radicals, and left-wing revolutionaries, a discourse that Nixon would successfully appropriate; that he was a key transitional figure between Barry Goldwater and Ronald Reagan; and that he was the victim of a deranged gunman in a Maryland shopping center in 1972. But I was wholly unprepared for Frady's compact, seamless narrative, the opening lines of which filled me with elation:

On a cold, rain-flicked night in 1967 a rickety twin-engine Convair 240 began a blind and uncertain descent through low clouds, abruptly breaking out over the scattered watery lights of Concord, New Hampshire. It came in headlong, less by instruments and calculation than with a precipitous lurching optimism. A damp huddle of greeters was waiting in the dark, and they waggled dime-store

Confederate flags when he emerged from the plane—a stumpy little man with heavy black eyebrows and bright black darting eyes and a puglike bulb of a nose who looked as if he might have stepped out of an eighteenth-century London street scene by Hogarth.

For me, *Wallace* remains, first and foremost, an incandescent portrait of a virtuoso American politician. Campaigning in a Birmingham shopping center in 1966, Wallace paused in the midst of a crowd before one man and inquired: "Yes, now, and how is Faye? Now, she was in St. Vincent's, wasn't she? Now, you tell her we gonna write her, heunh?" An old crony from Wallace's hometown mused to Frady: "He don't have no hobbies. He don't do any honest work. He don't drink. He ain't got but one serious appetite, and that's votes."

Frady approached *Wallace* as a nonfiction version of Robert Penn Warren's *All the King's Men*—"a tale of the methodical, relentless, and inexorable progression of a political Snopes, with a dauntless, limitless, and almost innocent rapacity, to the threshold of our most important political office." A young liberal with a vigorous commitment to racial equality, Frady undoubtedly loathed Wallace's politics; but there is nothing shrill or polemical in his rendering of the Alabama governor. Instead, Frady, in novelistic fashion, brought his subject to life with uncanny flair, and with considerable affection and sympathy. (Frady himself wrestled with fiction throughout his life, but never published a novel.) The book is dedicated to his editor at *Newsweek*, Joe Cumming—"under whom I learned that the highest journalism is informed by the insights of the poet and the artist"—and the qualities Frady attributed to Cumming were also the nerve center of his own modus operandi: "Instinctively he brings, to the hectic combustions of events, a most delicate sense of the dynamics of life, the most exquisite perceptions, a Dickensian relish for character, and a grace and vitality of language that approaches magic."

The special radiance of *Wallace* also owes much to Frady's avoidance of cant derived from rigid political frameworks, and he must have gazed with derision upon much of the blustery prose that flowed from left-wing quarters in the 1960s. His ambition was to create kaleidoscopic works of art along the lines of what Faulkner achieved in literature, Norman Mailer in nonfiction, and Tom Stoppard in drama. But he was also a sly, resourceful reporter who clocked the necessary hours with Wallace's inner circle of advisors and cronies. Says historian Dan Carter, who has written extensively about Wallace, "They assumed Frady was a good old boy, and they took him in."

Wallace has an intensely visual quality, and it is packed with marvelous set pieces, beginning with an atmospheric account of Wallace's excursion to Dartmouth College in 1967, where he "paced restlessly" on the stage before a packed audience, "exhilarated by the violence heavy in the air." During the speech, students stormed the podium—"led by a young professor with fine-spun hair and a freshly scrubbed cherubic complexion." Later, protestors assaulted Wallace's car while he reposed inside the vehicle with his cigar, "as small and still and inert as a rabbit in a burrow while hounds swirl and bay in the grass around it."

In a dreamy, fuguelike manner that recalls Faulkner and Penn Warren, the narrative plunges backward in time to Wallace's youth in Barbour County, Alabama. Following a "Huck Finn boyhood," Wallace entered the University of Alabama in 1937—"a small, quick, wiry youth, as thin as a ferret, with a cardboard suitcase and a quality of impatient, exuberant, ferocious hunger"—where his "amorous gusto" and his campus political machinations attracted attention. In 1942, he enlisted in the U.S. Army Air Forces, but his mind was mostly concentrated on politics, not warfare. Frady's quasi-anthropological excursions through Alabama, and his remarkable ear for vernacular speech, yielded a vast number of full-bodied anecdotes, including this one from a Barbour County farmer who recalled getting Christmas cards throughout the war from someone named "George C. Wallace":

> I thought it was real nice of this young fella, but I wasn't quite sure
> I knew who this George C. Wallace was, and why he was writin'
> me. It seemed kinda strange. Anyway, when the war was over with
> and the local political races had done got started over the county, I
> was out in my field one fine spring afternoon plowin', and I happen
> to look up and see this young fella comin' across the plowed field
> from the road, steppin' real smart and lively across those furrows,
> already grinnin' and his hand already stretched out, and all of a sudden I knew why I'd been gettin' them nice cards every Christmas.

In 1958, Wallace, who began his career as a New Deal liberal, and who would always remain an economic populist, ran for governor against one John Patterson, who won the support of the Ku Klux Klan while Wallace was left clutching the endorsements of the NAACP and some Jewish groups. After losing by 65,000 votes, Wallace strolled into a Montgomery hotel and informed a "smoky and clamorous" room of politicians: "John Patterson out-nigguhed me. And boys, I'm not goin' to be out-nigguhed again." In 1962, pandering to the racial anxieties of Alabama's whites, Wallace crushed his opponent, and before the inauguration privately confided, "I'm gonna make race the basis of politics in this state, and I'm gonna make it the basis of politics in this country." In 1963, black students tried to integrate the University of Alabama, an endeavor that attracted the attention of Robert Kennedy at the Justice Department, who pressured Wallace to lift the racial restrictions. Wallace instantly grasped the political rewards he'd gain if he defied the Kennedys, and as the crisis reached its apogee, he mumbled to some cronies: "By god, you watch now, they gonna send federal troops all over this state. We gonna be under military occupation."

Wallace is suffused with a bleak humor that intensifies as the book unfolds. In 1966, Wallace unveiled one of his most audacious political schemes: when term limits prevented him from running again for governor, he thrust his ailing wife, Lurleen, into the race, and she won a decisive victory. Still, the fact that Lurleen was running Alabama, and not him, left Wallace in a state of unease. Frady reproduces a salty exchange conveyed to him by one of Wallace's lieutenants in the wake of Lurleen's ascension: "I told him, 'George, you better start sleepin' with that woman.' He said, 'Yeah. Wouldn't it be a helluva note if she runs me off?' Back when he was governor, every time she'd call him up at the office, he'd say, 'What the hell you want? I'm busy now, don't be botherin' me.' But he's even talkin' sweet to her on the phone now."

One chuckles at this, but not for long. *Wallace* has an exceedingly wide (and expertly modulated) emotional register, and we soon see the former governor in the hospital with Lurleen—"a quiet, still, dwindled figure, a small wraithy spectre bundled in shawls." Frady writes: "On a soft and sweetly flushed May evening, about thirty minutes after midnight, she expired—Wallace glancing up from her slight form in the bed and snapping to the doctor, 'Is she gone?'" Wallace himself would soon be struck down: The revised edition of the book recounts "that glaring May afternoon in Laurel, Maryland, when suddenly he was lying spilled on the pavement of a shopping-center parking lot, half-curled like a dropped and dying squirrel."

Confined to a wheelchair, Wallace would famously repudiate his racial hate-mongering, and when Frady's book reaches its climax in 1979, we see him inside Martin Luther King Jr.'s sanctuary in Montgomery, declaring to the congregation, as strains of "Amazing Grace" fill the room: "In a way that was impossible before I was shot, I think I can understand something of the pain that black people have had to endure."

Wallace, who died in 1998, remained a ghostly presence in Frady's oeuvre. Near the end of his biography of Jesse Jackson, we glimpse Jackson, himself running for president, visiting Wallace in Montgomery a decade earlier:

> Wallace [was] aging and gnarled and reportedly given to moments of remorseful weeping over his blusterous racial rancors in the sixties, with Jackson now swallowing up his lumpy little paw of a hand in his own capacious grip and conducting a prayer for his "healing and health," and Wallace blurting out, "Jesse, thank you for coming. And I love you. . . ."

Excluding his stint for ABC News in the 1980s, Frady, who came to lament the ephemeral nature of television journalism, devoted his energies to book writing. His stirring biography of Billy Graham appeared in 1979, and *Southerners*, which is currently out of print, was published the next year. In 1996, Random House published Frady's biography of Jesse Jackson, which is one of the five or six most electrifying books I've read. Much of the material in *Jesse* originally appeared in *The New Yorker*. Still, by the time his final book came out in 2002—a slim but affecting biography of Martin Luther King Jr. in the Penguin Lives series—Frady was more or less invisible to the critical establishment, the serious reading public, and young writers. For a man who possessed a deep reservoir of pride, it wasn't easy to bear.

How did Frady come to be eclipsed by such New Journalistic stars as Norman Mailer, Tom Wolfe, Gay Talese, Joan Didion, and Michael Herr? Perhaps he was destined, like the columnist Murray Kempton or the novelist James Salter, to be a "writer's writer," whose work was mostly unappreciated by the public, but who remained an object of reverence and fascination to other writers, including Mailer, who sent a rousing message to Frady's memorial service in Manhattan in November 2004. It's not that

Frady, in his prime, lacked the support of influential critics and publications. In 1979, Elizabeth Hardwick insisted that *Wallace* and *Billy Graham* were "outstanding works of literature, not quite like any other in their intention and quality." Reviewing *Southerners* a year later, Robert Sherrill averred: "There are scenes here that Robert Penn Warren and Truman Capote couldn't improve on."

Halberstam attributes Frady's career difficulties to a variety of factors: his refusal to pander to the literary marketplace ("he did not have a great commercial touch"); his turbulent personal life ("he was a world-class romantic . . . much given to falling in love with love and marrying a bit too often"); and his nonchalance about financial matters ("when he got a wonderful $100,000 advance for his book on Billy Graham, his first instinct was to throw an immense party"). And then there was the prose itself—lush, musical, sometimes baroque and forbidding, full of linguistic acrobatics and lengthy sentences laced with adjectives and adverbs. "His books are the opposite of a quick read," says Gerald Howard, who edited *Southerners* for New American Library. "You have to enjoy the style as well as the subject." Quite true: none of Frady's works has the narrative engine of Capote's *In Cold Blood*, Mailer's *The Executioner's Song*, or Talese's *Thy Neighbor's Wife*. Frady's prose could be "sentimental or even incoherent," Sherrill wrote. "But when he brings it off, ah, the hair on your neck will stand up."

Frady moved to Los Angeles in 1987, and remained there until 2004, when he accepted a teaching position at Furman University, his alma mater in Greenville, South Carolina. He died, at sixty-four, a few weeks before he could teach his first class. I met him once, at a sparsely attended bookstore event in Manhattan in 2002, when he was on the road promoting his biography of Martin Luther King Jr. The swarthy good looks of his youth had dissipated under the weight of his illness, but his melodious Southern drawl was intact, and when he read a passage about King's slaying in Memphis, I felt the hair on my neck stand up. Afterward, I approached him with an armful of his old books. Seated at a table, wearing an elegant cream-colored suit, his bearing somewhat stiff and formal, Frady flipped through the pages, lingering over the annotations I had scrawled in the margins. When he looked up, there was a glint in his eye and a conspiratorial half-smile on his lips. He reached for a pen and inscribed each dog-eared volume: "best regards" . . . "vibrant regards" . . . "voluminous regards." And finally: "To Scott, one of the intrepid, Marshall."

Gal Beckerman

———

RIAN MALAN'S
MY TRAITOR'S HEART

Rian Malan's one and only meeting with J. M. Coetzee took place in the early 1990s. Malan greatly esteemed his fellow South African writer, and when Coetzee won the Nobel Prize in 2003, he declared that the laureate had "described, more truly than any other, what it was to be white and conscious in the face of apartheid's stupidities and cruelties." But what had struck Malan when he came face to face with Coetzee was, as he told the *New Statesman* in 1999, his asceticism. Coetzee was "a man of almost monkish self-discipline and dedication. He does not drink, smoke or eat meat. He cycles vast distances to keep fit and spends at least an hour at his writing-desk each morning, seven days a week. A colleague who has worked with him for more than a decade claims to have seen him laugh just once."

The writer is always a result of the man. With Coetzee, this intensity of focus and denial of his own ego have allowed him to create characters whose internal conflicts are perfectly attuned to those of white South Africa. From *Waiting for the Barbarians* to *Disgrace*, his novels are complex allegories in which psychology is presented not in its messy, everyday incarnation, but under the intense magnification of the author's microscope. His protagonists are invented for the specific purpose of illustrating a moral crisis.

I'm not saying that Coetzee's characters are representational stick figures. But they don't seem like people you would sit down with to drink a beer. Rian Malan, on the other hand, does seem like such a person—you might take a drag from his cigarette too. Yet his moral crisis was no less acute than Coetzee's. And in his only book, *My Traitor's Heart*, published just as the drama of apartheid's final demolition was taking place in 1990, Malan's project was no different from Coetzee's. He meant to answer the question posed in his epigraph, taken from a Boer reggae song: "How do I live in this strange place?"

My Traitor's Heart was as much the result of Malan's character as Coetzee's work was the result of his. Malan was and still is charismatic and rakishly good-looking, a drinker, loved by women, and obsessive in his intellectual pursuits. He wrote his book at the age of thirty-five, after years of traveling the world and living a hobo's existence. Not much has changed since then. A recent *Guardian* profile described him as living on various friends' couches. In 2005, he released an album of himself singing original folk songs, which the British paper described as a "part Tom Waits, part Serge Gainsbourg, all in Afrikaans."

But Malan hasn't produced another book. Since the publication of *My Traitor's Heart*, he has mostly attached himself to crusades. In 2000, he wrote an investigative piece about Solomon Linda, the Zulu singer who composed the original version of "The Lion Sleeps Tonight" ("Mbube"), only to be shortchanged of royalties when the song became an international classic. Malan's most recent obsession—disputing the official tally of people living with AIDS in South Africa—even cost him his marriage.

Yet, after all these years, *My Traitor's Heart* has lost none of its emotional power. Whereas Coetzee's novels have always felt like finished products, Malan's memoir was one of process: the book embodied his own struggle to see his country and its people as they actually were, and not as he wished them to be. To read it now is to experience the bravery of a young writer determined to stare unblinkingly at the ambiguity and complexity of what he found around him—including his own racism.

Born in 1954, Malan grew up in the liberal, northern, white suburbs of Johannesburg, where opposition to apartheid rule was taken for granted. He was quick to absorb the values of this milieu. After reading a *Life* magazine article about Che Guevara in Bolivia, he decided that he too wanted to be a Communist and help the persecuted blacks, though he never actually came into contact with any beyond the servants in his home. When he lost his virginity to a black woman whose name he never learned, it was a point of pride, to be bragged about at school. He even had a blues band and sang about black oppression.

"Isn't that absurd?" Malan writes in *My Traitor's Heart*.

Nobody laughed. We were utterly oblivious to the irony of it, which says something significant about those English-speaking, bourgeois, northern suburbs. They were in South Africa, but somehow not really of it. The rest of the country was a racist Calvinist despotism, but the northern suburbs were liberal, permissive, governed by the ruling philosophical orthodoxies of the West.

But Malan could not so easily escape the Afrikaner legacy. It was embedded in his name. A Malan, he wrote, "has been present at all the great dramas and turning points in the history of the Afrikaner tribe." His great-uncle, Daniel François Malan, was a major architect of apartheid during his tenure as prime minister, which ended the same year Rian was born. And even while the author was growing up, a Malan was the minister of defense. The family name was frequently and angrily evoked in the streets of the townships: "Voetsek, Malan!" ("Fuck off, Malan!")

The first hundred pages of *My Traitor's Heart* are pure memoir, gliding down the straits between the Boer history of Malan's name and his own constructed identity as a "Communist." Straight out of high school, he got a job working the crime beat for *The Star*, which at the time was the largest daily in South Africa. Being a journalist for one of the liberal big-city papers was as close as one could get to being a revolutionary without actually manning the barricades.

"Almost every day, I tucked my spiral notebook in my pocket and ventured forth to study the way South Africans killed each other," Malan recalls. It took him out of the bubble in which he had grown up and introduced him to his own country—to all its people, to black men he was able to respect and see as equals, but also to men he feared. When the Soweto riots erupted in the summer of 1976, Malan was overwhelmed by the violence of the black response. It forced him to confront his own allegiances. He was against apartheid and for black freedom, but he was also terrified of joining in their fight, and terrified of the hatred directed at him from even his new black friends.

Just then he was conscripted into the army. The two-year dispensation from mandatory military service he had received from the newspaper had run out. Malan decided that he had to leave. In *My Traitor's Heart*, he could have passed off this decision as a brave act, a rejection of the regime, but instead he writes:

> I ran because I wouldn't carry a gun for apartheid, and because I wouldn't carry a gun against it. I ran away because I hated Afrikaners and loved blacks. I ran away because I was an Afrikaner and feared blacks. You could say, I suppose, that I ran away from the paradox.

Malan spent the next few years in exile, traveling around Europe and eventually the United States, where he worked odd jobs and usually presented himself as a banished Afrikaner dissident. But he could not escape the paradox of his relationship to South Africa. It troubled him and would not let him become someone else.

Meanwhile, in 1984, P. W. Botha's parliamentary reforms—which gave the vote to "coloreds" (those of mixed race) and Asians, but still not to blacks—ignited violent protests all over South Africa, which would continue intermittently for the next several years. Malan could no longer stay on the sidelines. So he did what any aspiring writer would do: he wrote a book proposal and shopped it around. The book would be a family history of the Malan clan, or as he described it later in a *Washington Post* profile, a "multiracial, generational saga . . . a Boer *Roots*."

The exile returned with his book deal. But he soon felt an "increasing sense of dismay that what I was writing about really wasn't relevant to this terrible drama." He needed to confront the country in all its complexity; he needed to confront himself. And the best way he knew to do that was to venture out as a crime reporter again, to "seek a resolution of the paradox of my South African life in the stories of the way we killed one another."

The second part of *My Traitor's Heart*, the bulk of the book, is a compilation of these tales. And it is here that Malan's reporting is instructive for any writer trying to find a way to capture the truth of a conflict without simply pitting one side's narrative against the other's.

Take the story of the Hammerman. In the early 1980s, the white residents of Zululand were terrorized by a series of murders that seemed to have emerged out of their darkest nightmares. Someone was sneaking into their homes late at night and bludgeoning them to death in their beds. The murderer, when he was finally caught, turned out to be thirty-five-year-old Simon Mpungose, a Zulu.

Malan was present at his trial, and like many others, initially viewed him as a clear-cut victim of apartheid. Declaring himself ready to die for his sins, Mpungose took the stand and, as Malan writes, gave "as moving and powerful an indictment of South Africa as had ever been spoken." Denied a chance at an education or a steady job, the accused had spent his life in and out of jail for petty theft, including a stint in the infamously brutal Barberton prison. Before his most recent parole, he had a dream telling him that it was his duty to smash the heads of white men—that this was his fate. So frightened was Mpungose by this vision that he asked the warden to deport him from South Africa, or even to keep him in prison. His request was ignored, and when he was released, he began his killing spree. The narrative seemed clear to Malan at first. A man made insane by the oppressive environment had been transformed into a murderer.

But then Malan ventured into Zululand to find out if there was a deeper truth to Mpungose—and discovered a dark and twisted family history that started with an act of incest. The murderer was undoubtedly oppressed by apartheid, but he was equally haunted by this transgression, which to the Zulu was a stain that could never be washed away. Mpungose, writes Malan, was "an abomination in the eyes of his own people: the son of a man who should have been strangled at birth." In short, there was far more to this story than what the white magistrate and jury could see in the courtroom. This is how Malan sums up the Hammerman:

> As I read the Hammerman's moving courtroom testimony, Simon sprang to life in my imagination, fully fleshed and three dimensional, a victim and a martyr, a potentially good man made monster by apartheid. And then I went into the hills, and ducked into the huts of Simon's kin and found myself in a parallel world, a kingdom of unconquered consciousness that had somehow proved invulnerable to the white man's guns, his corruptive culture, and his truculent missionary faith. . . . Who was the Hammerman? In the end, I could not say.

What could possibly conclude this sad but passionate book? The third and final section of *My Traitor's Heart* is a parable: the story of Neil and

Creina Alcock, white South Africans who decided that they would live in Africa on Africa's terms, making a home in a parched region of Zululand called Msinga. There they devoted their lives to creating a cooperative farm and revitalizing the arid landscape.

By the time Malan went to visit, looking for answers, Neil had already been killed while trying to broker a truce between two local warring tribes. All the farm work had come to naught. Malan found the thin, weathered widow living in a mud hut, persisting in spite of all these setbacks. And Creina's life offered a sliver of a solution to Malan's paradox. He was forced to see that he had always been two people, "a Just White Man appalled by the cruelties Afrikaners inflicted on Africans, and an Afrikaner appalled by the cruelties Africans inflicted on each other, and might one day inflict on us. There were always these two paths open before me, these two forces tugging at my traitor's heart." The example of Creina Alcock, who had taken "the path that led into Africa, the path of no guarantees," did not seem easy or even desirable. But Malan came to the conclusion that it was the only real path open to him.

In the end, it is Creina's words that serve as a fitting coda for the book, and anticipate the relative stability of postapartheid South Africa, which nobody could have imagined during the turmoil of 1986: "Trust can never be a fortress, a safe enclosure against life. Trusting is dangerous. But without trust there is no hope for love, and love is all we have to hold against the dark."

My Traitor's Heart angered many people in South Africa, both black and white. The author spared no one. He was seen as both a self-hating Afrikaner and a self-admitted racist. For Malan, this was the only way to come to terms with his country and with himself: to find a way to live in that strange place. What his book still provides today is an example of how to write about the strange places, those that cannot be easily represented, that are too often perceived as one thing or another, but are really both. *My Traitor's Heart* was most definitely the work of a young man. Malan ranted and raged in its pages. But he never abandoned the idea that there was a paradox in South Africa's history, and that truth resided in wrestling that paradox to the ground and staring it in the face.

Is there a stranger place for Western eyes than Africa? Even those writers and journalists who don't have the tortured connection to the continent that Malan has—or especially those who don't—tend to describe it in simple terms. It is a place of goodness, of noble savages, or one of darkness, disease, and war. In neither case is the continent seen for what it is. Too often, it acts as little more than a backdrop against which the Westerner finds or loses himself. Malan understood the problem and tried desperately to cut through this self-imposed blindness. His insight about the Mpungose trial could be applied to most people writing about Africa:

> This is the trouble with white people in my country. Our eyes are sealed by cataracts against which our white brains project their chosen preconceptions of Africa and Africans. Some whites see danger, some see savagery, some see victims, and some see revolutionary heroes. Very few of us see clearly.

Very few of us see clearly. Malan tried, and his book is an expression of just how painful the attempt can be. This might be why he has never written another one, nor attempted anything quite as ambitious or personal as *My Traitor's Heart*. Unlike Coetzee or Nadine Gordimer, who have also written with honesty about the white person's place in Africa, Malan declined to don a fictional mask: he put *himself* on the examination table, let it get messy, scrutinized his conscience just as he did those many corpses. After all that, and after discovering that he must remain attached to a place that will forever try to spit him out, what more could he say?

John Maxwell Hamilton

VINCENT SHEEAN'S
PERSONAL HISTORY

On a dreary day in October 1922, a young man from Pana, a small town in southern Illinois, walked into the Paris office of the *Chicago Tribune*. In experience, he scarcely came up to the knee of most journalists. There had been a stint at the *Chicago Daily News*, from which he was fired; a few months covering scandal for the New York *Daily News*; and a few months more in Europe, writing the greater part of a novel that was eventually lost. Now Vincent Sheean needed a job and hoped to find one at the *Trib*, which hired him as a utility man for its Paris newspaper and for the Paris bureau of its foreign service. "In a click of time, I became what was called a 'foreign correspondent,'" he later wrote in *Personal History*.

The six-foot, two-inch James Vincent Sheean—"Jimmy" to his friends and "Vincent" to the *Tribune* editors, who nixed the idea of a "J. V. Sheean" byline—was never inconspicuous, even at the University of Chicago, from which (in keeping with his early career) he did not graduate. A classmate, John Gunther, described Sheean in awestruck terms: "He hummed Mozart, wore green pants, and spoke better Italian than the Italian professors." But for all his panache, Sheean was not the only hopeful young journalist walking the streets of Paris in the 1920s and 1930s. Would-be foreign correspondents "rolled up in waves," as an editor at the *Paris Herald* put it, in that city and throughout Europe. Some of the most important names of twentieth-century journalism—Gunther, Eric Sevareid, William Shirer, and Dorothy Thompson, to name just a few—wandered in the way Sheean did, as cubs, and left as lions.

What elevated Sheean even among luminaries in journalism was the literary quality of his reporting, his uncanny ability to situate himself in the slipstream of monumental news, and the intensity of feeling with which he viewed those events. All of that is on display in *Personal History*, published thirteen years after he found his job at the *Tribune*. For correspondents who stood witness to events rushing the world to war, Sheean's chronicle became a defining narrative. And although the book is largely forgotten, it is still a potential beacon for journalists seeking to recover the purpose and credibility they see slipping from their hands today.

* * *

Sheean's first decade or so of foreign correspondence, the framework of *Personal History*, was a tutorial in world news. He covered the Separatist revolt in the Rhineland, the League of Nations Assembly in Geneva, the early days of Mussolini's fascist state in Rome, and Primo de Rivera's Spain, where he was arrested. In Morocco, Riff rebel leader Abd el-Krim was willing to talk to any correspondent who managed the hazardous trip past Spanish or French forces to reach him. Donning a turban and a loose-fitting *jellaba*, Sheean finagled passage through the French lines and returned to Tangier under a hail of Spanish bullets.

Sheean wrote a book about the adventure, *An American Among the Riffi*, and a year later made the behind-the-lines trip once again. From there he went to Persia for the installation of the new Shah, Reza Pahlavi, who had knocked his predecessor off the Peacock Throne; to China, where Chiang Kai-shek's Nationalist forces consolidated their hold on the country and ousted their Communist partners; to Moscow for the tenth anniversary of the revolution, an event marked by Stalin's arrest of Trotsky; and to British-controlled Palestine, where in August 1929 Arabs clashed with Jews bent on creating their own state.

Between the first and second Riff adventures, Sheean and the *Tribune* parted company. The circumstances of his exit remain both murky and typical of that paper. Colonel Robert McCormick, the newspaper's proprietor, gave Sheean a fancy dinner to celebrate his triumph and safe return from Morocco. Not long afterward, the star reporter was fired. Mc-

Cormick subsequently wrote to his cousin, Joseph Patterson, that Sheean was "suspected of bad practices. I have forgotten whether he left the Foreign News Service or was fired." Sheean himself was unfazed. He would not have stayed long, even if the mercurial colonel had been steadfast in his admiration. Sheean's motto, after all, which he recorded in a 1946 diary entry, was "My own job in my own way."

We forget how many outlets freelance correspondents had in the interwar years. Sheean wrote for *Asia* magazine and the North American Newspaper Alliance, which serviced a number of American dailies. Both used him extensively, but without monopoly. His reporting, along with short fiction, appeared in *The Atlantic Monthly*, *Harper's*, *Woman's Home Companion*, *Collier's*, *Century*, *Saturday Evening Post*, *Commonweal*, and *The New Republic*. In France between assignments, he worked for another English-language Paris newspaper, the *Times*, which lacked circulation and revenue, but not talented journalists. The newspaper appeared to have correspondents everywhere—in fact, its clever staff more or less imagined what was happening abroad, and wrote it with authority. In between this and more travel in Europe, Sheean wrote another book of reporting, *The New Persia*, and his first published novels.

Sheean's swashbuckling adventures in the Riff brought him a Richard Harding Davis sort of fame. Rumors circulated during the first trip that he was killed; on the second, he was supposedly shot as a spy. As useful as this was to his career, Sheean was impatient with superficial thrill-seeking, as well as "professional indifference to the material of journalism." Davis, in his *A Year from a Reporter's Notebook*, found coronations and wars "interesting"—a word he liked quite a lot. For him, these were merely events without any profound significance. But Sheean dove below the surface of the news to seek its meaning. It was this quest that energized *Personal History*, which ended this way:

> Even if I took no part in the direct struggle by which others attempted to hasten the processes that were here seen to be inevitable in human history, I had to recognize its urgency and find my place with relation to it, in the hope that whatever I did (if indeed I could do anything) would at last integrate the one existence I possess into the many in which it had been cast.

The decade in which I had pursued such a conclusion through the outer storms had ended, and I was on my way back to a civilization that could never again be so sure of itself, never again so blind.

Personal History, Sheean wrote in a preface to a later edition of the book, "is, I suppose, a hybrid form, and is neither personal nor historical but contains elements of both." In one way, the book was all about him. His experiences appeared on every page. Yet the autobiographical tone was deceptive. Much of his life was left out or obscured. The focus was on the events he witnessed. His persona was that of a self-deprecating guide. He could be any American searching for answers to the pressing political and social questions of the day.

A poignant foil in this drama was the beautiful revolutionary Rayna Prohme—another young American who also happened to be from Illinois. Sheean met Prohme in Hankou, China, where he had gone in 1927 as "your plain seeker-after curiosity . . . tending, more and more, to treat the whole of the visible universe as a catering firm employed in his service." This industrial city had become the base for Communist operations after Chiang Kaishek gained control over most of China and purged leftist elements from his government. Prohme worked for Mikhail Borodin, an agent of the Comintern, the Soviet Union's organization for promoting revolution abroad.

Sheean fell deeply, if platonically, in love with Prohme and her commitment to Communism, about which they sparred for hours. After Hankou fell, Sheean smuggled Borodin's wife out of the country. Prohme and Sheean subsequently met again in Moscow. Hers, he wrote, was "a marvelously pure flame, and even though I clearly could not hope to share its incandescence, it seemed to me that I must hover as near it as possible." When she died of encephalitis in 1927, some seven months after they met, Sheean wept and drank disconsolately. He would go on to dedicate *Personal History* to her, and the concluding section of the book was an imaginary conversation with the deceased woman.

* * *

When *Personal History* appeared in early 1935, the praise was nearly universal. Mary McCarthy, known for her acid reviews in *The Nation* and elsewhere, pronounced Sheean "a human being of extraordinary taste and sensibility, who throughout fifteen years of turbulent experience has been primarily interested in moral values." Malcolm Cowley, literary editor of *The New Republic* and a fellow sojourner in Paris, thought "the most impressive feature of the story is that besides being an extraordinarily interesting personal document, it is also, by strict standards, a work of art. . . . This autobiography, with a few names changed to give it the appearance of fiction, would certainly rank among the good novels of this decade."

Bookstore sales were as enthusiastic as the critical reception. *Personal History* was the fourth best-selling nonfiction title of the year. And when the National Book Awards were inaugurated in 1935, *Personal History* won in the biography category. Not long afterward, producer Walter Wanger purchased the film rights. The resulting movie appeared in theaters as *Foreign Correspondent* (1940), directed by Alfred Hitchcock. Although much rewritten to keep up with political events in Europe, the theme of the independent journalist willing to take a stand was pure Sheean, and the film was nominated for an Academy Award for Best Picture.

Personal History became a journalistic sun that drew other correspondents into its gravitational field. In the past, correspondents either wrote colorfully of their adventures, as Sheean had about his exploits in the Riff, or produced desiccated tomes on foreign affairs, one of the most erudite examples being Paul Scott Mowrer's *Our Foreign Affairs*. In *Personal History*, Sheean showed how to be both engaging *and* serious, an approach that was perfect for a time when fearful Americans were desperate to make sense of the world. In 1937, two years after *Personal History* appeared, *Saturday Review of Literature* editor Henry Seidel Canby scanned the shelf of recent books by foreign correspondents. He pronounced Sheean's the archetype of a new genre that sought "to break through the crust of the news to see what lies underneath."

This was saying quite a lot, as many correspondents' memoirs had received rave reviews. In 1936, the year after *Personal History* appeared, three memoirs by foreign correspondents showed up on the list of the ten most successful nonfiction books of the year. One was *The Way of a Transgressor* by Negley Farson, who was identified by his *Chicago Daily News* colleagues as a "combination of Childe Harold and Captain from Castile." The second was *I Write as I Please* by *The New York Times*'s Walter Duranty, the doyen of the Moscow correspondents. The third, *Inside Europe*, was by another *Chicago Daily News* reporter, Sheean's classmate John Gunther. None of these personal histories was exactly like Sheean's, whose prose, insight, and intensity were difficult to match. But he was the touchstone. United Press correspondent Mary Knight, author of *On My Own*, had "joined the parade," wrote a reviewer, after Sheean "set so many worn portable typewriters clacking." The dustjacket of UP reporter Webb Miller's *I Found No Peace: The Journal of a Foreign Correspondent* proclaimed: "Like Vincent Sheean's *Personal History*, another absorbing biographical record of an American newspaper correspondent." John T. Whitaker's *And Fear Came*, Robert St. John's *Foreign Correspondent*, Quentin Reynolds's *A London Diary*, Shirer's *Berlin Diary*, and Sevareid's *Not So Wild a Dream*—the last two best-sellers—picked up Sheean's métier, as did scores of others.

"Sheean established, as had nobody before him, that what counts is what a reporter thinks," observed fellow correspondent Kenneth Stewart of the books that followed as "extensions and refinements" of *Personal History*. "I should guess that no book published in our time had a greater direct response from the working press itself or gave the public better insight into a newspaperman's mind." John Gunther put it more simply: Vincent Sheean was "the father of us all."

Through the rest of the 1930s and the war, there wasn't a media door that Sheean could not walk through. He authored more novels; translated Eve Curie's biography of her mother, *Madame Curie*, and Benedetto Croce's *Germany and Europe: A Spiritual Dissension*; and wrote a play, *An International Incident*, for actress Ethel Barrymore. He continued to report for newspapers and magazines, as well as on CBS radio with Edward R. Murrow in London, and produced three more memoirs, which he wanted to title *Personal History II, III*, and *IV*, but ended up as *Not Peace but a Sword* (1939), *Between the Thunder and the Sun* (1943), and *This House Against This House* (1946).

The emotional intensity that continued to suffuse Sheean's books was not a literary put-on. As far as he was concerned, those imaginary conversations with Prohme were real—and ongoing. "I see her, Bernie," he blurted out to a colleague, while they sat drinking in a Paris bistro. "There she is. There's Rayna." Sheean conversed with her while his companion looked on. Nervous breakdowns and wild drinking were mixed with eerily accurate premonitions, the most spectacular of which was his prediction that Gandhi was going to be assassinated by one of his own kind, a Hindu. With credentials from *Holiday* magazine, whose range of interests belied its title, Sheean went to India. A few days after he arrived in early 1948, a fanatic Hindu fatally shot the Mahatma while Sheean stood a few paces away. Afterward, he wrote *Lead, Kindly Light*, which mixed his experience with a study of Gandhi's spiritual life.

As happened with so many correspondents, when Cold War certitudes about Communism drove out other questions, Sheean's fame faded. By 1949, when *Lead, Kindly Light* appeared, not one of the ten top-selling books for the year was by a journalist, let alone a foreign correspondent. The public was hungry for lighter fare: three of the top sellers were how-to books about winning at canasta, and another was Norman Vincent Peale's *A Guide to Confident Living.* "One wonders," wrote a reviewer of *This House Against This House*, "if this type of intimate, first-person journalism hasn't about outlived its usefulness as a serious contribution to world thought."

It is a question still worth pondering.

For the modern reader, *Personal History* celebrates a lost golden age of foreign correspondence. News outlets were plentiful. The dollar was strong and the cost of living abroad cheap. Americans were well liked. Editors could not yet reach a reporter on the steppes of Russia by pressing a few telephone buttons. In those days, American correspondents enjoyed great freedom, and large numbers of them spent years abroad, roving and learning. When it came to foreseeing the impending World War II, Sheean wrote, "International journalism was more alert than international statesmanship." This self-confidence makes for a poignant contrast with our current pop-cultural image of the foreign correspondent, a disheveled figure most often freighted with angst. "It's not a fucking forties movie," says a character in *The Killing Fields*. "You can't just get on a goddamn plane and make the whole world come out right."

We cannot bring back that era. But in a world in which our security is threadbare and questions abound about what is happening and why, the need for foreign reporting is no less urgent—and Sheean's approach no less compelling.

The drive for credibility has pushed journalists toward greater caution. When *USA Today* correspondent Jack Kelley was found to have fabricated news, the home-office solution was to double-check quotes in reporters' stories and comb expense accounts to see whether they had been where they said they were. Such scrutiny may avoid more Kelleys (or it may not). But it does not encourage correspondents to interpret the world for an audience that often doesn't have the background to weigh a leader's quote or judge the relevance of a distant fact.

For all its emotion, Sheean's approach was more objective than the pseudo-scientific artifices of attributing all insights and opinions to others and of balancing unequal points of view to avoid seeming "biased." Like a proper scientist, Sheean brought expert observational skills to his reporting—he told the reader what he saw, the conditions under which he saw it, and what it meant.

That was strikingly apparent in 1938, when Sheean covered Germany's annexation of Austria for the *Herald Tribune*. He rejected the widespread argument that the Nazis succeeded by terror alone. The party's message, argued Sheean in the paper's banner story of July 5, had mass appeal: "I am unable to name any sources or any authority for what I say, since nobody in Vienna is willing to be quoted, but investigations in the last ten days have given me one firm belief—that nothing will shake the power of National Socialism here until it has completed its historic functions and has reached its natural and inevitable conclusion in general war."

This was not the antiestablishment free-for-all of the New Journalism that emerged in the 1960s. Nor was it the self-centered blogging of today. It was informed reporting of the highest order.

Journalists of a certain age remember Sheean. As I was working on this article, long-retired CBS correspondent Marvin Kalb mentioned that he read *Personal History* when it came out and said to himself, "I've got to be a journalist." May it inspire a new generation of correspondents as well.

Tom Piazza

NORMAN MAILER'S
THE ARMIES OF THE NIGHT

Early in Norman Mailer's *The Armies of the Night: History as a Novel, the Novel as History*, the poet Robert Lowell tells Mailer that he thinks of him as "the finest journalist in America." One writer's compliment is plainly another's backhanded insult. Mailer had a lifelong ambivalence about his reportorial, as opposed to his novelistic, work, considering fiction to be a higher calling. "There are days," Mailer responds, tartly, "when I think of myself as being the best writer in America."

A year after Mailer's death in November 2007, at eighty-four, maybe we can begin to be grateful that he worked both sides of the yard. He was always an interesting and ambitious novelist, yet Mailer's loyalties were divided between his fictive imagination and his fascination with the way society works. At his best, the two merged, and the results made for some of the most extraordinary writing of the postwar era.

When Mailer died, commentators lined up to bemoan the dearth of serious writers who, like Mailer, were willing to match their own egos, their own perceptions and sensibilities, against large contemporary events. We suffer from no shortage of gutsy reporters eager to cover trouble spots around the world. But rarely does that kind of journalistic impulse coexist with a personally distinct literary style, an ability to use one's own point of view as an entry into the reality of a subject. For Mailer, that subjectivity was not just a stylistic trait but a kind of ethical tenet, the door into a larger—he would call it novelistic—truth.

Mailer brought this approach to its peak in *The Armies of the Night*. His journalistic mock epic of the 1967 March on the Pentagon first appeared in *Harper's*, occupying the cover and taking up practically the entire issue, and came out in book form in the spring of 1968. By that time, the so-called New Journalism was in full bloom; Tom Wolfe, Gay Talese, Hunter S. Thompson, Joan Didion, George Plimpton, Truman Capote, and others had already done significant work, bringing highly individual styles and sensibilities to a form that had stubbornly held to its conventions of objectivity.

The Armies of the Night stood out from all their work in some important ways. Most New Journalism focused on a subculture—motorcycle gangs, hippies, Hollywood celebrity—and, by rendering it vividly, attempted to make inductive points about the larger culture. Mailer had a different approach. He got as close as he could to the gears of power, and then used his own sensibilities as a set of coordinates by which to measure the dimensions of people and events on the national stage: presidents and astronauts, championship fights and political conventions.

He had shown this predilection before writing *Armies*. There was his *Esquire* article about John F. Kennedy at the 1960 Democratic convention, "Superman Comes to the Supermarket," and "In the Red Light," a piece on the 1964 Republican convention. There was also the audacious interstitial writing, addressed directly to Kennedy, the new President of the United States, in one of his most interesting and neglected books, *The Presidential Papers*. But in *Armies*, Mailer upped the ante by placing himself at the center of the narrative, turning himself into a self-dramatizing (in the purest sense of the phrase) protagonist. He gave his consciousness not just eyes but a face.

The book presents Mailer as a reluctant participant in a mass protest against the Vietnam War that took place in October 1967. A cast of extraordinary characters populates the stage—Robert Lowell, Dwight Macdonald, Paul Goodman, Ed DeGrazia—along with a secondary crew of protesters, marshals, homegrown Nazis, police, court bailiffs, and Mailer's fourth wife back in New York City. The author also manages to cram a lot of action into the short span of the narrative. He delivers a drunken speech on the eve of the march, attends a party full of liberal academics, consorts with Lowell, Macdonald, William Sloane Coffin Jr., and other notables gathered for the march, participates in the protest itself, gets arrested, and spends the night in jail.

The publication of the first part of the book in *Harper's* created a sensation. A month later, the book's second part, a shorter and more formal account of the planning and execution of the march, was published in *Commentary*. They were combined in the finished volume, to which Mailer appended his subtitle, *History as a Novel, the Novel as History*. It was immediately and almost universally recognized as a "triumph," to use Dwight Macdonald's word, and went on to win both the National Book Award and the Pulitzer Prize.

* * *

Mailer's most significant discovery in *Armies* was the technique of writing about himself in the third person, as if he were a character in a novel. "Norman Mailer," the character, is treated as a mock-heroic protagonist making his way through a complex network of competing interests and sensibilities during that weekend in Washington. Because we get a vivid sense of him early on, we gladly accept the topspin he puts on his perceptions as he serves them up.

He earns a powerful narrative leverage, starting with the very first sentence. "From the outset," he writes, "let us bring you news of your protagonist." This lone sentence is followed by an extended excerpt from *Time*'s snarky report on Mailer's preprotest monologue at the Ambassador Theater.

It is a shrewd and effective opening gambit. There is a clearly stated "us" and "you," so an immediate dramatic relation is set up between the narrative voice and the reader. The voice is bringing us "news"—we love news!—and it is about "your" protagonist, drawing us into a subliminal complicity. Within a page we learn that the "us" who is bringing the news is, in fact, our protagonist himself, a man of many parts, apparently, perhaps containing Whitmanesque multitudes.

The *Time* excerpt is studded with value judgments masquerading as straight reporting: the upcoming march is referred to as "Saturday's capers," and Dwight Macdonald, who shared the stage with Mailer, is "the bearded literary critic." When the excerpt is done, Mailer quits this curtain-raiser with a single sentence, "Now we may leave *Time* in order to find out what happened." We are hooked. And we have been introduced to the book's underlying principle: the notion that a reporter who is willing to characterize events without first characterizing himself or herself is inherently suspect. One can't approach the truth without first turning an eye on one's own subjectivity.

The second chapter, the book's official beginning, puts this principle into practice immediately. "On a day somewhat early in September," the narrative begins, "the year of the first March on the Pentagon, 1967, the phone rang one morning and Norman Mailer, operating on his own principle of war games and random play, picked it up. This was not characteristic of Mailer. Like most people whose nerves are sufficiently sensitive to keep them well-covered with flesh, he detested the telephone. Taken in excess, it drove some psychic equivalent of static into the privacies of the brain."

Since we know that we are hearing this from Mailer himself, we are, again, complicit in the narrative; a game is in progress, and we are being shown the rules. We are going to get our events via a mind that is nothing if not subjective, and yet paradoxically objective about its own subjectivity. We will get descriptions of action (he picks up the ringing phone), background context for the action (it was not characteristic), observations delivered from an unexpected angle with a Mark-of-Zorro flourish (the oversensitive nerves with their sheathing of flesh), and an insistence on sharp detail in metaphor (the static being driven into "the privacies of the brain"). The author will juggle these ingredients in quick succession, always with huge linguistic gusto.

Mailer's prose obsessively amends its own perceptions, makes parenthetical observations, qualifies, anticipates, demurs, constantly tries to stand outside itself. He was, in fact, a species of performance artist, discovering metaphors en route and mingling them with dazzling audacity. Here he is, riffing on his discomfort at a party thrown by some liberal backers of the march: "The architecture of his personality bore resemblance to some provincial cathedral which warring orders of the church might have designed separately over several centuries. . . . Boldness, attacks of shyness, rude assertion, and circumlocutions tortured as arthritic fingers working at lace, all took their turn with him, and these shuttlings of mood became most pronounced in their resemblance to the banging and shunting of freight cars when he was with liberal academics." If your sensibilities are ruffled by a mixed metaphor, comic grandiosity, or long sentences, steer clear of Mailer.

Through it all, Mailer is crucially aware not just of his own motivations, but of how they might play to the public. "Mailer," he writes, "had the most developed sense of image; if not, he would have been a figure of deficiency, for people had been regarding him by his public image since he was twenty-five years old. He had, in fact, learned to live in the sarcophagus of his image—at night, in his sleep, he might dart out, and paint improvements on the sarcophagus. During the day, while he was helpless, newspapermen and other assorted bravos of the media and literary world would carve ugly pictures on the living tomb of his legend."

One would be tempted to find a new name for this point of view—first person third, perhaps—and think of it as a technical innovation, but for two facts. Mailer winks at the first of these facts upon awakening in his hotel, the Hay-Adams, on the morning of the march, then never mentions it again. "One may wonder," he writes, "if the Adams in the name of his hotel bore any relation to Henry." Yes, one may, but nobody need wonder afterward where Mailer got the idea of writing about himself in the third person. By alluding to the author of *The Education of Henry Adams*, Mailer tips his hat, and his hand, to his fellow Harvard alumnus and consummate insider/outsider. *The Education*, published in 1918, may lack Mailer's bravado and sheer joy in language, but it does use the same first-person-third technique to locate its author in an ambiguous social and historical position. (Adams's book, by the way, also won a Pulitzer, presented posthumously in 1919.)

The other fact is that innovations, if they are indeed innovations, typically spawn techniques useful to succeeding practitioners of the form. But the technique of *The Armies of the Night* is so completely suffused with Mailer's personality, his peculiar mix of ego and charm, of self-regard and self-deprecation, his intelligence and occasional clumsiness, that subsequent attempts by other writers to use the first person third have inevitably read as embarrassing, inadvertent homages.

* * *

Mailer recognized early on, before a lot of writers, that politics—most of contemporary public life, in fact—was turning into a kind of theater. Actions on the political stage had a symbolic weight that often outbalanced what might previously have been thought of as their practical consequences. This development was the wedge that eventually drove an unbridgeable divide between the Old Left, with its programmatic preoccupations and endless appetite for dogma, and the New Left, with its vivid sense of the theatrical. It was also the subtext of the 1967 march. The real dynamics of public life were shifting away from the old tabulations of political give-and-take. Instead, the cut of a candidate's suit or the unfortunate presence of his five o'clock shadow would travel out over the television sets of the nation and affect people's perceptions on a level that bypassed any substantial argument.

The media, to use Mailer's terminology, were driving public events deeper and deeper into the "privacies" of every citizen's brain, short-circuiting linear thinking in favor of image-driven manipulation. And this was precisely why traditional reportage had become ill-equipped for locating the truth of "what happened." What we needed, insisted Mailer, was a different approach: "The novel must replace history at precisely that point where experience is sufficiently emotional, spiritual, psychical, moral, existential, or supernatural to expose the fact that the historian in pursuing the experience would be obliged to quit the clearly demarcated limits of historic inquiry." His book, he adds, "while still written in the cloak of an historic style, and, therefore, continuously attempting to be scrupulous to the welter of a hundred confusing and opposed facts, will now unashamedly enter that world of strange lights and intuitive speculation that is the novel."

Needless to say, this development dovetailed perfectly with Mailer's own impulses. And yet (and this is perhaps Mailer's most important saving grace), he was deeply ambivalent about it. Highly sensitive to the theater of events and personae, Mailer was alive to the ways in which the manipulation of surfaces could, and would, be used to deaden the public's ability to think, to sift and evaluate information. Writers, public officials, advertising people, politicians, speech writers—all were in possession of a dangerous weapon, and they were obliged to use it with singular care. "Style," Mailer wrote, much later, in an introduction to a book by Carl Oglesby, a former member of Students for a Democratic Society, about the JFK assassination, "is not the servant of our desire to inform others how to think, but the precise instrument by which we attempt to locate the truth."

In the light of today's endemic spin, such a sentiment would seem a touching artifact of a simpler time, if it weren't so achievable by any individual sitting alone in a room trying to locate the truth. The prerequisite is the sense that it is both possible and desirable. Citizen Mailer turns the act of seeing, the workings of consciousness itself, into the ultimate civic act—a responsibility shared by everyone in the privacies of his or her brain. There is something profoundly democratic in his insistence that the individual's sensibility could meet the largest events on equal terms, with one's own centering and irreducible humanity as the common denominator.

* * *

As a writer and as a man, Mailer was always in a state of tension. His mind and heart were planted in a wholly American flux—improvisatory, protean, deeply ambiguous in intention, supremely egotistical and supremely civic-minded. These tensions give his work its deepest dynamism, turning it into a theater of opposing psychic forces. At the same time, Mailer was not quite a wholly American spirit. Or perhaps his Americanness existed in extraordinary tension with his respect for European intellectual and artistic traditions. When, toward the end of *Advertisements for Myself*, he promises to write a novel worthy of being read by "Dostoevsky and Marx; Joyce and Freud; Stendhal, Tolstoy, Proust and Spengler; Faulkner, and even old moldering Hemingway," 80 percent of the honor roll has been read before an American is mentioned.

Mailer retained an almost sentimental attachment to the novel form, yet his major gift was not the ability to imagine living, three-dimensional fictional characters. What he did have a genius for was dramatized dialectic. He loved to interview himself; his 1966 collection *Cannibals and Christians* contains three self-interviews, and more followed through the years. The form of *Armies* is itself a kind of dialogue, in two halves, between two different modes of discourse.

In every sense—stylistic, cultural, political—he was stretched between two worlds. Never programmatic enough for the Old Left, neither was he ever anarchic enough to fully sign on to the New Left's Grand Guignol. Although at times Mailer liked to characterize himself as the Devil (or at least *a* devil) while criticizing America's "Faustian" ambitions, he was far from Goethe's "spirit that negates." Rather, he found in his own Hebraic, and specifically Talmudic, tradition (his grandfather was a rabbi) perhaps his deepest conviction: the sense that there is something central, necessary, and even sacred in doubt, in the nuanced weighing of competing intellectual and moral and spiritual claims. And this allowed him to put his own ego, his outsized talents, his brilliance and narcissism, in the service of a higher calling. Because of that, *The Armies of the Night* remains one of the most enlivening, and most deeply American, testaments ever written.

Thomas Mallon

WILLIAM MANCHESTER'S
THE DEATH OF A PRESIDENT

The first printing of William Manchester's *The Death of a President* ran to a half million copies and reached stores in April 1967. I believe I bought mine with several weeks' worth of my allowance, though perhaps it was a sixteenth birthday present. Whatever the case, so definitive was the book believed to be that I felt prompted to start composing my own epilogue on one of the volume's blank endpapers: "November 7, 1967—Former Vice-President John Nance Garner, born November 22, 1868, died in Uvalde, Texas. He received Kennedy's second to last phone call on his 95th birthday."

Annotating a clothbound book constituted a big step up in literary luxury for me. Truman Capote's *In Cold Blood*, published the previous year, and the last book to be a national event on the scale of Manchester's, had sent me to my town's little rental library (itself already something of an anachronism). My early perusal of Capote's creation, for perhaps a nickel a day, provoked the jealousy of my English teacher. Even so, my possession of the first "nonfiction novel" was only temporary. The Manchester book was mine, and its 710 pages have been on my shelves for more than 40 years.

Latter-day evidence that Capote's book contained rather more fiction than its author let on has rendered it more controversial with the years:

along with two movies of it, two more *about* it have been made. Manchester's book is no longer much read, and the prepublication fracas over it is largely forgotten. And yet, at the time, the book gave rise to an emotional and widely publicized battle of editors, lawyers, and public images, one that put Manchester into the hospital for nervous exhaustion (Bayer Aspirin offered him an endorsement deal) and left many Americans ready to relinquish Jacqueline Kennedy, their so recently revered tragic heroine, to the hairy, moneyed grip of Aristotle Onassis.

In and of itself, *The Death of a President* remains, even at this long remove, a work of considerable fascination. It is startlingly evocative. It is also much more modern and much worse written than one remembers—or, in my youthful case, realized.

* * *

What Manchester years later called "the longest presidential obituary in history" was authorized by Robert and, even more crucially, Jacqueline Kennedy. "I think Jackie picked me because she thought I would be manageable," the author reflected during the mid-1970s, in an essay called "Controversy." Manchester had, after all, produced an admiring book called *Portrait of a President* during John F. Kennedy's time in the White House, and gone so far as to allow JFK a look at the galleys. In "Controversy," he admits that "authorized history may be a poor idea," while reminding the reader that his selection by Kennedy's widow and younger brother assured him the cooperation of almost everyone, from cabinet members to the president's valet.

Manchester would end up paying a very high price for all this access. Yet it helped make possible the book's genuine intimacy and power, qualities that further depended on Manchester's own instinct for both telling detail and the emotional core of each narrative line. The prologue, for example, contains a brilliant, extended reconstruction of Kennedy's last evening in Washington—Wednesday, November 20—when a reception for members of the judiciary filled the East Room. About 55 hours and 400 pages later, the reader will see candlesticks and crêpe being brought into the same room, as it awaits the arrival of the president's coffin. Among other particulars: Sargent Shriver, the president's brother-in-law, gets the Washington, D.C. Highway Department to provide some of the little flame pots that they used to use to mark off nighttime road-repair work. The pots arrive by 3:30 a.m. to line the walkway of the mansion, just ahead of a squad of marines in dress blues, all of them chagrined by the knowledge of "where Lee Harvey Oswald had learned to shoot."

In between the book's East Room scenes, one experiences not just the violence of the shooting, but two tremendous dramas that went unreported on November 22. First, there is the legal and physical struggle at Parkland Hospital between Kennedy's men and the Dallas County coroner, who didn't want to release the president's body without an autopsy (presidential assassination was not yet a federal crime, and Texas had jurisdiction). Mirroring this turf war is the bitter forced proximity of what Arthur Schlesinger called "loyalists" (grief-stricken lieutenants of the dead president) and "realists" (those improvising assistance to the new one). What happened aboard Air Force One, on the tarmac at Love Field and then in the skies between Dallas and Washington, is the heart of Manchester's book and his chief contribution to history. Johnson felt that the panicked conditions of the Cold War required an immediate swearing-in; some of the Kennedy people found his haste unseemly. Godfrey McHugh, JFK's preening Air Force aide, was lucky he wasn't court-martialed for pointing to Kennedy's coffin and saying, "I have only one president, and he's lying back in that cabin."

Nothing was too small for Manchester's attention, and he put it all to chilling, if sometimes top-heavily ironic, use. He considered Kennedy's driver's license and the twenty-six dollars in the president's wallet; consulted the notebooks of reporters who'd been present for Air Force One's arrival an hour before the shooting; tracked other patients receiving treatment in the emergency room of Parkland Hospital when Kennedy arrived; talked to the Dallas-based Secret Service agent who had also guided Franklin Roosevelt's car through the city twenty-seven years before; investigated the roost of pigeons on the roof of the Texas School Book Depository. The texture is so fine-grained that it's difficult to discern what rule of thumb relegates certain details to the book's footnotes while other minutiae remain in the regular text.

Manchester was working in the period when writers like Tom Wolfe and Jimmy Breslin—Capote too, for that matter—were giving New Journalism its gaudy birth. *The Death of a President* is, of course, a work of history, by an author reconstructing rather than participating in events. Still, the history is so recent and the techniques so similar to Wolfe and Co.'s that one wonders why Breslin's piece about the digging of Kennedy's grave has become a textbook example of the genre while Manchester goes unmentioned in Marc Weingarten's study of New Journalism, *The Gang That Wouldn't Write Straight.*

Manchester's book is otherwise replete with instructive reminders about the relative modernity, and primitivism, of news reporting in 1963. The new Telstar satellite may have helped to spread word of the president's murder with what seemed futuristic speed, but Manchester also shows us two wire-service reporters fighting over a single car telephone on the way to Parkland Hospital. As the assassination weekend wears on, the author seems to forecast our blogging and Twittering present when he notes: "The number and variety of Americans who were keeping written accounts of their impressions is striking."

Manchester is especially good at stripping away later knowledge from the characters in his story, thus letting them behave with a suspenseful immediacy on the page. He picks his peripheral figures shrewdly, turning mere extras into developed, if minor, characters. Sergeant Bob Dugger, for example, looks like "a poster of police brutality" during the standoff at Parkland. In fact, the "bull-necked" Dallas patrol officer is a fellow Navy veteran and believer in integration who voted for Kennedy in 1960. At the hospital he stands next to the First Lady, choked with grief and reticence, wishing that he instead of JFK were dead, until he at last bursts into tears and manages to offer Mrs. Kennedy his name. It's a stupendous little scene.

Alas, Manchester's overwriting—as inadvertent as Tom Wolfe's was deliberate—can reach grotesque extremes. Trapped in their limousine amid the gunfire, Oswald's victims "lay entangled in their abbatoir." The assassin didn't kill, he "slew," while a cigarette that's being smoked is seen "shrinking to its doom." If another book has ever made multiple uses of the word "debouched," I've yet to read it. The diction throws up one risible roadblock after another: "apopemptic," "comminated," "vermiculating," "atrabilious." Maybe all this helped me with my SATs back in 1967, but in 2009 I find myself skipping to the next paragraph instead of reaching for a dictionary.

The language, so weirdly puffed up and perfumed, seems almost a form of grief, some strange, Pentecostal utterance that's the opposite of what poor Sergeant Dugger was suffering. Metaphors are either baffling ("as obvious as a Parcheesi board") or tormented through extension, and the tone can be crazily uncertain, as in one passage where Manchester twists himself into a combination of Cotton Mather and Mickey Spillane. He is attempting to explain why the tony New Frontiersmen could never have understood the sleazy world of Jack Ruby, Oswald's killer:

> The men and women who had surrounded President Kennedy . . . were unacquainted with the maggoty half-world of dockets and flesh-peddlers, of furtive men with mud-colored faces and bottle blondes whose high-arched overplucked eyebrows give their flat glittering eyes a perpetually startled expression.

During his battle with Bobby and Jackie Kennedy, Manchester's editors would betray him in the largest way possible, sticking up for the writer's subjects instead of the writer. But they also let him down line by un-blue-penciled line.

* * *

When *The Death of a President* was released in 1967, public confidence in the Warren Report was only beginning its long slide down the Grassy Knoll. Manchester dismissed the possibility of conspiracy in the space of two footnotes. His contempt and anger toward Oswald are so keen that he can barely allow the assassin onto the page. To the author, Kennedy's killer is a head case ("he was going mad") whose Marxist politics are too puerile for consideration, and who can be dismissed as "barely literate." In fact, though painfully dyslexic, Oswald was a serious reader whose library borrowings in the summer of 1963 included Manchester's *Portrait of a President*.

Manchester remains, then, what students of the assassination call an LN (Lone Nutter), as opposed to a CT (Conspiracy Theorist). However, he belonged to a large liberal sect of Lone Nutterism that believed a city-wide atmosphere of political malice had prodded Oswald toward his explosion. Dallas, with its fiercely right-wing ethos, is more or less made into the killer's codefendant.

Over and over, the author suggests what he calls "a plural responsibility for the tragedy," and quotes others who spoke in the same vein. Ralph Dungan, a special assistant to President Kennedy, remarked that "the hell of it is, they'll blame it all on that twenty-four-year-old boy," while David Brinkley declared on network television, as JFK's coffin was lowered into the ground, that "the act which killed the president was spawned out of bigotry and extremism." The city's tendencies toward both were marked.

That they led Lee Harvey Oswald to kill John F. Kennedy—seven months after he nearly succeeded in killing General Edwin Walker, the most celebrated right-wing extremist in Dallas—is no more clear today than it was in 1967. Nor is it any clearer now whether the myriad cheering spectators for Kennedy's Dallas motorcade should assume or escape a share of the "plural responsibility."

And yet, for all this collective guilt, much of the emotional drive in *The Death of a President* comes from a simple sense that a big man has been killed by a little one, a king cut down by a serf. Camelot imagery for the Kennedy years sprang not from Manchester but from Theodore H. White (with a conscious assist from Jackie Kennedy). Nonetheless, *The Death of a President* has enough of its own royalist trappings and machinery to have put off some who read it in manuscript. The main divisions of the text are organized under the characters' Secret Service code names—JFK is "Lancer," while Mrs. Kennedy is "Lace"—and the murder happens because the protagonists must make a kind of royal progress, waving from their carriage in all their sexual glamour, through the inhospitable province where some of their vassals have been feuding. The warring factions and egos within the Texas Democratic Party thus hasten the end of a "dazzling three-year reign" whose closing moments take place against a backdrop decidedly unfit for a king and queen. The author winces in describing "the automotive nature of the landscape" (too many gas stations) and even "the tawdry Hertz clock" above the Texas School Book Depository. (Never mind that the Hertz rental-car business may have been made possible in part by the president's father, who during the 1920s manipulated stock in the Yellow Cab Company with his friend John Hertz.)

Manchester tells us that John F. Kennedy, whose "great heart continued to pump" against all odds in the emergency room, was a reader not only of Thucydides but also, when aboard Air Force One, the Bible: "On flights alone the President had read it evenings before snapping off the night light." Perhaps he did. But a plaster sainthood hardens very quickly around JFK once he ceases to propel Manchester's narrative with his own words and deeds.

With Mrs. Kennedy, it's a different story. Manchester may hymn the First Lady's looks and elegance, but in her he has a living—indeed, suddenly metamorphosing—creature to deal with. After the killing, immune to Scotch and sedatives, she marshals her will for a series of history-minded decisions and truly graceful gestures (gently touching the ham hand of the weeping Sergeant Dugger, for one). Manchester makes plain that Bobby Kennedy, not his sister-in-law, took the initial steps toward planning the massive state funeral. But once Mrs. Kennedy rose to full function, the two of them became a formidable team.

In 1966 they united against Manchester, attempting to thwart serialization of *The Death of a President* in *Look* magazine, and then to block publication of the book itself by redeeming the author's early, unwise promise of "manuscript approval." In Mrs. Kennedy's case, Manchester realized, the basic problem was that "she didn't really want any book" at all on the assassination, especially one that had been enabled by her long, daiquiri-driven interviews with the author. When she met with Manchester to hash things out, she deployed "tears, grimaces, and whispery cries of *'Jesus Christ!'*," as well as a threatening reminder that the only thing the American public wouldn't put up with from her was running off with Eddie Fisher.

Bobby Kennedy's objections followed a political calculus that now seems obscure. Not yet having decided to run for president, he was afraid that Manchester's depictions of Lyndon Johnson—first as a humbled vice president and then, suddenly, an overeager chief executive—might create problems for himself inside the Democratic Party. Evan Thomas, Manchester's editor at Harper & Row (and father of RFK's subsequent biographer), proposed a bundle of cuts and changes, not only to please the Kennedy family but to keep Harper & Row from losing a crack at LBJ's own memoirs when the time came for them to be auctioned.

Any reader of the battle scenes between the Kennedy "loyalists" and Johnson "realists" will understand that Manchester's portrait of Johnson is in fact so fundamentally reasonable and sympathetic—it shows a man marshaling his huge skills during what, for all anyone knew, might be an international plot preceding a nuclear attack—that it has to have been largely that way from the beginning. On the other hand, those in the Kennedy camp (including, occasionally, RFK himself) behaved so disgracefully that one must wonder if Bobby's real fear wasn't what readers would think of *them*. In this sense, Robert Kennedy's attempt to suppress Manchester's book seems only an extension of the grief-entitled arrogance on display that weekend.

* * *

At the beginning of this decade, I made my own foray into the history of the assassination with a long profile for *The New Yorker* of Ruth Paine, the

Quaker woman in Dallas who became a key Warren Commission witness because of her solicitous friendship with Lee and Marina Oswald. In the nine months before Kennedy's murder, Ruth helped Oswald to get his job at the Book Depository and remained unaware that he was keeping a rifle in her garage.

A poignant figure whose life was convulsed by her connection to the killing, she left Manchester, as he put it in a footnote, "impressed by her exceptional forthrightness." He sought her out primarily for help in understanding Oswald's behavior. When I tracked Ruth down decades later, it was not in order to reinvestigate the crime (I am an implacable Lone Nutter), but with a view toward understanding her own character and ordeal. Among my many sources were Manchester's book as well the notes from his interview with Ruth, now in the National Archives.

I have come to realize that Manchester's approach—his quest for the smallest particulars, his emotional sense of history and its ironies—informed my work more than any specific facts I learned from him. When it came time to publish *Mrs. Paine's Garage* (2002), an expansion of my magazine piece, I endured nothing to equal Manchester's legal and personal ordeal, but I did experience a degree of psychological stress. Ruth's own agitation about having revisited her awful experience spilled over into my life and, predictably, I had to deal with a bilious bubbling up of scorn from the still feverish swamps of conspiracy theory.

I was pleased to learn that Manchester had read what ran in *The New Yorker*. He told me so during our only meeting, in the spring of 2002, just after he had been awarded a National Humanities Medal for his career as an historian. Manchester was in a wheelchair, two strokes having left him unable to finish the third volume of his biography of Winston Churchill. He spoke with difficulty, but managed to tell me one story that suggested the years of strain he endured while producing his flawed, distinguished, and essential book. In the summer of 1964, he explained, he had conducted two interviews with Oswald's bizarre, money-mad mother, Marguerite, at her little house in Fort Worth, Texas. Despite her derangement, she surely sensed the level of his regard for her son. And as he left her for the last time, she uttered her defiant *envoi*: "You can't say my son wasn't a good shot!"

Manchester told me this story at a White House reception for the Humanities medalists, just down the hall from the East Room.

Miles Corwin

GABRIEL GARCÍA MÁRQUEZ'S
THE STORY OF A SHIPWRECKED SAILOR

In 1955, eight crew members of a Colombian naval destroyer in the Caribbean were swept overboard by a giant wave. Luis Alejandro Velasco, a sailor who spent ten days on a life raft without food or water, was the only survivor. The editor of the Colombian newspaper *El Espectador* assigned the story to a twenty-seven-year-old reporter who had been dabbling in fiction and had a reputation as a gifted feature writer: Gabriel García Márquez.

The young journalist quickly uncovered a military scandal. As his fourteen-part series revealed, the sailors owed their deaths not to a storm, as Colombia's military dictatorship had claimed, but to naval negligence. The decks of the *Caldas* had been stacked high with television sets, washing machines, and refrigerators purchased in the United States. These appliances, which were being ferried to Colombia against military regulations, had caused the ship to list dangerously. And because the *Caldas* was so overloaded, it was unable to maneuver and rescue the sailors. In addition, the life rafts on board were too small and carried no supplies, and the navy called off the search for survivors after only four days.

By the time the series ended, *El Espectador*'s circulation had almost doubled. The public always likes an exposé, but what made the stories so popular was not simply the explosive revelations of military incompetence. García Márquez had managed to transform Velasco's account into a narrative so dramatic and compelling that readers lined up in front of the newspaper's offices, waiting to buy copies.

After the series ran, the government denied that the destroyer had been loaded with contraband merchandise. García Márquez turned up the investigative heat: he tracked down crewmen who owned cameras and purchased their photographs from the voyage, in which the illicit cargo, with factory labels, could be easily seen.

The series marked a turning point in García Márquez's life and writing career. The government was so incensed that the newspaper's editors, who feared for the young reporter's safety, sent him to Paris as its foreign correspondent. A few months later the government shut *El Espectador* down. The disappearance of his meal ticket forced García Márquez into the role of an itinerant journalist who sold freelance stories to pay the bills—and, crucially, continued to write fiction.

The relatively spare prose of the Velasco series bears little resemblance to the poetic, multilayered, sometimes hallucinatory language that would mark García Márquez's maturity as a novelist. Still, the articles—which were published in book form as *The Story of a Shipwrecked Sailor* in 1970, and translated into English sixteen years later—represent a milestone in his literary evolution. "This is where his gifted storytelling emerges," says Raymond Williams, a professor of Latin American literature at the University of California, Riverside, who has written two books about the author. Prior to the series, he suggests, García Márquez had been writing somewhat amateurish short stories. Now, says Williams, he was rising to the challenge of constructing a lengthy narrative: "The ability he has to maintain a level of suspense throughout is something that later became a powerful element of his novels."

* * *

In fact, it was the reporter's capacity to anatomize human behavior—rather than simply pass along the facts—that first drew García Márquez to the newsroom. He was a young law student with little interest in journalism when an acquaintance named Elvira Mendoza, who edited the women's section of a Bogotá newspaper, was assigned to interview the Argentinean actress Berta Singerman. The diva was so arrogant and supercilious that she refused to answer any questions. Finally, her husband intervened and salvaged the interview.

For García Márquez, this was a revelation about the possibilities of journalism. As he wrote in his autobiography, *Living to Tell the Tale*, which appeared in English in 2003:

> Elvira did not write the dialogue she had foreseen, based on the diva's responses, but instead wrote an article about her difficulties with Berta Singerman. She took advantage of the providential intervention of the husband and turned him into the real protagonist of the meeting. . . . The sangfroid and ingenuity with which Elvira . . . used Singerman's foolishness to reveal her true personality set me to thinking for the first time about the possibilities of journalism, not as a primary source of information but as much more: a literary genre. Before many years passed I would prove this in my own flesh, until I came to believe, as I believe today more than ever, that the novel and journalism are children of the same mother. . . . Elvira's article made me aware of the reporter I carried sleeping in my heart and I resolved to wake him. I began to read newspapers in a different way.

García Márquez ended up leaving law school and working for a series of Colombian newspapers. He spent most of his early career writing movie reviews, human-interest stories, and a daily, unsigned column he shared with other reporters that resembled *The New Yorker*'s "Talk of the Town"—a common feature of South American newspapers. Yet he aspired to cover more substantive issues, including politics and government corruption, and to pursue investigative projects.

When he was first hired at *El Espectador*, García Márquez hoped to impress an editor by the name of Jose Salgar. "It seems to me that Salgar had his eye on me to be a reporter," he later recounted in his autobiography, "while the others had relegated me to films, editorials, and cultural matters because I had always been designated a short-story writer. But my dream was to be a reporter . . . and I knew that Salgar was the best teacher." The editor taught him to how to communicate his ideas clearly and pare down his florid prose. Every time Salgar read one of García Márquez's stories, he made "the strenuous gesture of forcing a cork out of a bottle and said, 'Wring the neck of the swan.'"

Soon, García Márquez was assigned the kinds of projects he had dreamed of pursuing. He wrote numerous in-depth stories, including pieces about the corruption surrounding the construction of a port on the Caribbean coast, the neglect of war veterans by the government, and landslides that killed dozens of people in a slum neighborhood. He specialized in what Latin American newspapers called the *refrito* ("refried"): a detailed reconstruction of a dramatic news event, published weeks or months later with élan and great narrative skill. And then something new landed on his desk: the Velasco series.

* * *

After Luis Alejandro Velasco washed ashore, he was lionized by the press, decorated by the Colombian president, and became a national hero. García Márquez thought it was absurd the way the government held up Velasco as an example of patriotic morality. What's more, he believed the sailor had sold out in a most unseemly manner—advertising the brand of watch he wore at sea (because it had not stopped) and the shoes on his feet (because they were too sturdy for him to tear apart and eat during his ordeal).

A month after his rescue, Velasco walked into *El Espectador*'s newsroom and offered the exclusive rights to his story. He had already told his tale to innumerable reporters as well as government officials, and the staff doubted he had anything new to add to the record. "We sent him away," García Márquez recalls in his autobiography. "But on a hunch, [Salgar] caught up with him on the stairway, accepted the deal, and placed him in my hands. It was as if he had given me a time bomb."

At first, though, García Márquez declined the assignment. He believed the story was not only a "dead fish," as he later wrote, but "a rotten one"—which is to say, both dated and dubious. Salgar persisted. "I informed him," García Márquez recounts, "that I would write the article out of obedience as his employee but would not put my name to it. Without having thought about it first, this was a fortuitous but on-target determination regarding the story, for it obliged me to tell it in the first-person voice of the protagonist."

García Márquez proved the newspaper adage that there can't be great writing without great reporting. Over the course of twenty consecutive days, he interviewed Velasco for six hours each day. To make sure his subject was telling the truth, he frequently interjected trick questions, hoping to expose any contradictions in Velasco's tale. "I sincerely believe that interviewing is a kind of fictional genre and that it must be regarded in this light," García Márquez wrote after his interviews with the sailor. He added:

The majority of journalists let the tape recorder do the work, and they think that they are respecting the wishes of the person they are interviewing by retranscribing word for word what he says. They do not realize that this work method is really quite disrespectful: whenever someone speaks, he hesitates, goes off on tangents, does not finish his sentences, and he makes trifling remarks. For me the tape recorder must only be used to record material that the journalist will decide to use later on, that he will interpret and will choose to present in his own way. In this sense it is possible to interview someone in the same way that you write a novel or poetry.

After 120 hours, García Márquez had a detailed, comprehensive account of Velasco's ordeal. The challenge was how to involve the reader in a saga that featured a single character who was alone for 10 days, floating aimlessly in a small raft.

The answer was a steady heightening of dramatic tension. In the first few pages of the book, he notes that before the destroyer shipped out of Mobile, Alabama, Velasco and some of his shipmates watched *The Caine Mutiny*, foreshadowing the disaster to come. The best part of the movie, Velasco tells García Márquez, was the storm. And the sheer realism of the sequence inevitably made some of the crew uneasy: "I don't mean to say that from that moment I began to anticipate the catastrophe," Velasco says, "but I had never been so apprehensive before a voyage."

Not overly subtle, perhaps, but certainly effective. García Márquez concludes each section with a Dickensian cliffhanger. He ends chapter 2, for example, with a dramatic description that compels the reader onward:

I started to raise my arm to look at my watch, but at that moment I couldn't see my arm, or my watch either. I didn't see the wave. . . . I swam upward for one, two, three seconds. I tried to reach the surface. I needed air. I was suffocating. . . . A second later, about a hundred meters way, the ship surged up between the waves, gushing water from all sides like a submarine. It was only then that I realized I had fallen overboard.

The next chapter begins with Velasco alone in the middle of the ocean. While García Márquez keeps his language relatively spare—he was writing for a newspaper, after all—there are frequent glimmers of the great descriptive powers that would later animate his novels. "Soon the sky turned red, and I continued to search the horizon," recalls Velasco (or at least Velasco being channeled by the young reporter). "Then it turned a deep violet as I kept watching. To one side of the life raft, like a yellow diamond in a wine-colored sky, the first star appeared, immobile and perfect."

* * *

Throughout the sailor's ordeal, García Márquez touches on themes that would consistently interest him for the rest of his career. In his early short stories, he had already explored the interior life of his characters, probing their dreams and sometimes surreal reveries. Yet these explorations felt anomalous—youthful stabs at insight without any real connection to the plot. In the Velasco series, he felt free to reconstruct his subject's interior monologues, and for the first time, they were actually integral to the narrative. And when the sailor sees mirages, or converses with imaginary companions, or struggles with the distortions of time, these passages presage the author's mature fiction.

Here, as he did later on, García Márquez also affirms his belief that narrative plays a significant role in people's lives. When Velasco finally washes ashore, after ten days in the open sea, a man wearing a straw hat comes upon him, with a donkey and an emaciated dog in tow. García Márquez relates the exchange between the two:

> "Help me," I repeated desperately, worried that the man hadn't understood me.
> "What happened to you?" he asked in a friendly tone of voice.
> When I heard him speak I realized that, more than thirst, hunger, and despair, what tormented me most was the need to tell someone what had happened to me.

Countless literary critics have written about how Ernest Hemingway's prose emerged from his journalism. Scholars have looked for a similar stylistic genealogy in the case of García Márquez. There are, of course, major differences between the two: García Márquez's language is more complex and poetic. Yet even his inimitable passages of magic realism are influenced by his years as a reporter, says Robert Sims, a professor of Spanish literature at Virginia Commonwealth University and the author of *The First García Márquez: A Study of His Journalistic Writing from 1948 to 1955*. The most surrealistic events are believable, Sims argues, because they are recounted in an objective, journalistic tone. And García Márquez first mastered this tone—in which magic always pays heed to realism—when he described Velasco's ordeal. "It's never melodramatic," Sims says. "He never lets Velasco get overwrought or maudlin or sink into total despair. García Márquez always cuts it off before it reaches that point. The tone is even and neutral, just like in *A Hundred Years of Solitude*."

Nor did he ever forget the reporter's obligation to hook readers with the very first sentence. Some of García Márquez's early newspaper leads read like fiction, and point directly to his later work. For example, he wrote a series for *El Espectador* about a swampy, disease-ridden area of Colombia near the coast, and opened with a lead guaranteed to intrigue any reader: "Several years ago a ghostly, glassy-looking man, with a big stomach as taut as a drum, came to a doctor's office in the city. He said, 'Doctor, I have come to have you remove a monkey that was put in my belly.'"

The reverse is true as well. In his novels and short stories, he often opens with indelible lines about death, many of which read like dramatic newspaper leads. Here he cuts to the chase and ensnares the reader with an elegant composure:

Many years later, as he faced the firing squad, Colonel Aureliano Buendía was to remember that distant afternoon when his father took him to discover ice. (*A Hundred Years of Solitude*)

On the day they were going to kill him, Santiago Nasar got up at five-thirty in the morning to wait for the boat the bishop was coming on. (*Chronicle of a Death Foretold*)

Since it's Sunday and it's stopped raining, I think I'll take a bouquet of roses to my grave. ("Someone Has Been Disarranging These Roses")

When Jose Montiel died, everyone felt avenged except his widow; but it took several hours for everyone to believe that he had indeed died. ("Montiel's Widow")

Senator Onesimo Sanchez had six months and eleven days to go before his death when he found the woman of his life. ("Death Constant Beyond Love")

Hemingway and García Márquez also differed on how lasting one's journalistic apprenticeship should be. The former admitted that journalism was good training for a young novelist, but contended that it was important to get out in time, because newspapers could ruin a writer. García Márquez felt otherwise. "That supposedly bad influence that journalism has on literature isn't so certain," he has said. "First of all, because I don't think anything destroys the writer, not even hunger. Secondly, because journalism helps you stay in touch with reality, which is essential for working in literature."

García Márquez put this belief into practice: even after he attained great success as a novelist, he never abandoned journalism. He used the money from his 1982 Nobel Prize to purchase *Cambio*, a failing weekly newsmagazine in Colombia. He established the Foundation for New Ibero-American Journalism, where veteran reporters give workshops for young Latin American journalists. And during the past few decades, while writing novels, he has kept reality at close quarters, publishing numerous essays, opinion pieces, articles, and a masterful book of reconstructive journalism, *News of a Kidnapping*. In the latter, he chronicled the abduction of ten prominent Colombians by Pablo Escobar, the head of the Medellín drug cartel, and his painstaking account of their eight-month ordeal might strike some readers as a protracted ensemble version of *The Story of a Shipwrecked Sailor*.

In any case, his breakthrough series went on to be one of his most popular books, selling about ten million copies, the majority of them in the original Spanish. To his readers, this apprentice work, with its early and exquisite balance of magic and realism, fit very comfortably into the author's canon. The fact that it was told in the first person may have actually made it feel more literary rather than less—a feat of modernist ventriloquism.

As for García Márquez himself, he had mixed feelings about the transformation of his newspaper series into a bona fide work of art—or at least a hardcover book. And in a new introduction he wrote, he seemed to betray some nostalgia for the days when he was simply a semianonymous reporter rather than an international brand name. "I have not reread this story in fifteen years," he wrote. "It seems worthy of publication, but I have never quite understood the usefulness of publishing it. I find it depressing that the publishers are not so much interested in the merit of the story as in the name of the author, which, much to my sorrow, is also that of a fashionable writer. If it is now published in the form of a book, that is because I agreed without thinking about it very much, and I am not a man to go back on his word."

David Ulin

―

JOAN DIDION'S
SLOUCHING TOWARDS BETHLEHEM

It was my mother, of all people, who introduced me to Joan Didion's *Slouching Towards Bethlehem*. This was in the early summer of 1980, when I was not quite nineteen and living, first with two friends and later by myself, in a studio apartment on Haight Street in San Francisco. My next-door neighbor was a jovial ex-biker turned dope dealer who shared his studio with a (very) young wife and a fifteen-year-old runaway. Downstairs lived a guitar player who had once jammed with the Grateful Dead. I was taking a year off between high school and college, and Haight Street was my own little slice of hippie paradise, rundown and edgy in ways that seemed glamorous to me.

Then as now, the streets of the district were populated by a motley crew of burnouts: street kids with rucksacks and rasta caps, and squatters living in the abandoned buildings on Masonic who came down to panhandle in front of Uganda Liquors. I was an outsider—a kind of cultural tourist, living in San Francisco for six months before returning to the regulated world I'd always known—and there was something about their hand-to-mouth existence that I allowed myself to believe was authentic, even free.

For my mother, I see now, this was a dangerous narrative. That the Haight was already dead, in the early summer of 1980, was beside the point; it was not the present that interested me. I was more concerned with the idea of recapturing something. It wasn't that I was ignorant. I understood what I thought to be the larger story, the way a romantic movement—the Haight of the early-to-mid-1960s—had been co-opted by the mainstream, a corruption so profound it had inspired the Diggers to stage a "Death of Hippie" funeral procession on Haight Street in October 1967.

I had read Tom Wolfe and Hunter S. Thompson. I knew the revolution had failed. In *Fear and Loathing in Las Vegas*, published in 1971, Thompson offered his own elegy for the era: "So now, less than five years later, you can go up on a steep hill in Las Vegas and look West, and with the right kind of eyes you can almost see the high-water mark—that place where the wave finally broke and rolled back."

And yet I observed the scene around me with no sense of context, no idea of what it meant. It was during my time in San Francisco that Ronald Reagan won the Republican nomination for president, and I can still recall watching his acceptance speech on television in a friend's apartment near the Marina, reacting as if it had not been the obvious outcome all along. When I think back on the moment, it is always with a pinprick of self-loathing for not having recognized Reagan as the inevitable reaction, the symbolic counterweight, to the hippie myth. That, of course, is another story. What's important is that I didn't *know* enough.

As it happens, this is precisely the point of *Slouching Towards Bethlehem*—both the collection and the long title piece, which recounts the author's experience in Haight-Ashbury in the weeks and months leading up to the Summer of Love. Published in 1968, this collection of magazine pieces is, on the most basic level, a reaction to its moment. Yet that is no longer where its power resides. Now we are drawn to its peculiar sense of cultural dissolution, which Didion weaves relentlessly through every piece.

Even at eighteen, I knew the Yeats poem from which she takes her title, and which she quotes in its entirety as an epigraph. "Things fall apart," Yeats writes, "the centre cannot hold." And, a few lines down: "The best lack all conviction, while the worst / Are full of passionate intensity." This is what caused my mother to press *Slouching Towards Bethlehem* on me. "Read the Haight-Ashbury essay," she repeated, her voice a little urgent over the long-distance wires, as if conveying a cautionary tale. And why not? For her, that's exactly what it was: a portrait not just of the dangerous territory in which, she feared, her son was treading, but also of the breakdown of a certain set of shared assumptions, a certain narrative.

Didion's collection opens with a searing essay called "Some Dreamers of the Golden Dream." It has become one of the author's iconic pieces, a model of the form. Still, for all that's been said about the essay, it's worth looking at again, both for how it sets up the rest of the book and how it establishes the key elements of Didion's authorial stance.

It is a story about a murder in which the crime and its protagonists are not even described until four pages have passed. At its heart is a tawdry domestic drama—the marriage of Gordon and Lucille Miller, a San Bernardino couple awash in debt and acrimony, which ends with Gordon being burned up in the back of the family Volkswagen, in a fire Lucille may or may not have set. For Didion, this is nothing short of a master metaphor, one rooted not only in the actual events but also in the Southern California noir tradition, "in which violence and threats and blackmail are made to seem commonplaces of middleclass life."

Didion is always attuned to the role landscape plays in human agency, to the exigencies and influences of place. And for her, place has everything to do with weather—or more broadly, what we might call the elements. Growing up in Sacramento, a delta city sustained by farming and protected from the adjacent river by a complex, New Orleans-style network of levees, she knows the risks of nature in her bones. That's clear from the opening lines of "Some Dreamers of the Golden Dream," with their invocation of the Santa Ana winds:

> This is a story about love and death in the golden land, and begins with the country. The San Bernardino Valley lies only an hour east of Los Angeles by the San Bernardino Freeway but is in certain ways an alien place: not the coastal California of the subtropical twilights and the soft westerlies off the Pacific but a harsher California, haunted by the Mojave just beyond the mountains, devastated by the hot dry Santa Ana wind that comes down through the passes at 100 miles an hour and whines through the eucalyptus windbreaks and works on the nerves. October is the bad month for the wind, the month when breathing is difficult and the hills blaze up spontaneously. There has been no rain since April. Every voice seems a scream. It is the season of suicide and divorce and prickly dread, wherever the wind blows.

What we're seeing is the creation of a narrative. It's a narrative of conditionality, of breakdown, in which the physical environment and the human environment can't help but reflect each other. Lucille and Gordon Miller are the perfect protagonists for such a tale: rootless, grasping, unable to believe in much of anything, not even (or especially) themselves. They have come to California looking for something. But as these opening lines make explicit, it is the wrong California, "the last stop for all those who come from somewhere else."

Here Didion exposes the underside of the great Golden State myth: that it is a land of reinvention, in which we escape the past to find ourselves. For the Millers (and by implication, countless others), it is a land of disconnection, in which we are not reborn but lost. Such a theme colors the whole of *Slouching*. It is there in "Where the Kissing Never Stops," a biting portrait of Joan Baez's Institute for the Study of Nonviolence in the Carmel Valley ("a place where the sun shines and the ambiguities can be set aside a little while longer, a place where everyone can be warm and loving and share confidences"). And it is there in the bleak, fulminating title essay, with its vision of Haight-Ashbury as the epicenter of a children's revolution:

> The center was not holding. It was a country of bankruptcy notices and public-auction announcements and commonplace reports of casual killings and misplaced children and abandoned homes and vandals who misspelled even the four-letter words they scrawled. It was a country in which families routinely disappeared, trailing bad checks and repossession papers. Adolescents drifted from city to torn city, sloughing off both the past and the future as snakes shed their skins, children who were never taught and would never now learn the games that had held the society together. People were missing. Children were missing. Parents were missing. Those left behind filed desultory missing-persons reports, then moved on themselves.

There is here a strong whiff of class consciousness, or an innate conservatism—or more accurately, a bit of both. It makes sense, given Didion's status as a former Goldwater Republican (she started out writing for the *National Review*) turned social observer in a culture collapsing inward on itself. This is the source of her cool, ironic distance: what she called, in a 2006 interview, her air of "triangulation."

She addresses the same topic in her preface to *Slouching*. "My only advantage as a reporter," she declares, "is that I am so physically small, so temperamentally unobtrusive, and so neurotically inarticulate that people tend to forget that my presence runs counter to their best interests. And it always does. That is one last thing to remember: *writers are always selling somebody out.*" This is, you could argue, the basic rule of journalism; like any reporter, Didion has to negotiate access, which she then uses to her own ends. But she is also talking about the larger picture, the round-robin of chaos and self-deception which permeates the book down to its smallest details.

Sometimes the chaos is explicitly political. In "Comrade Laski, C.P.U.S.A. (M.-L.)"—the very title of which makes trenchant sport of the tortured fragmentation of the 1960s radical left—she profiles the twenty-six-year-old "General Secretary of the Central Committee of the Communist Party U.S.A. (Marxist-Leninist), a splinter group of Stalinist-Maoists who divide their energies between Watts and Harlem." Despite this tongue-twister of a title, Michael Laski strikes Didion as a boy terrified of chaos, living in "an immutably ordered world." Comrade Laski, she observes, "had with him a small red book of Mao's poems, and as he talked he squared it on the table, aligned it with the table edge first vertically and then horizontally. To understand who Laski is you must have a feeling for that kind of compulsion. One does not think of him eating, or in bed."

There's no mistaking the judgment in that description, just as there is no mistaking the sense that Lucille Miller's greatest sin isn't that she may have murdered her husband (Didion remains remarkably nuanced on that issue), but that she comes from the wrong side of the tracks. Yet the author recognizes something of herself—something of her inner weather—in the young apparatchik:

As it happens I am comfortable with the Michael Laskis of this world, with those who live outside rather than in, those in whom the sense of dread is so acute that they turn to extreme and doomed commitments: I know something about dread myself, and appreciate the elaborate systems with which some people manage to fill the void, appreciate all the opiates of the people, whether they are as accessible as alcohol and heroin and promiscuity or as hard to come by as faith in God or History.

I know something about dread myself. The phrase reverberates throughout her entire body of work. "You are getting a woman who somewhere along the line misplaced whatever slight faith she ever had in the social contract, in the ameliorative principle, in the whole grand pattern of human endeavor," Didion writes in her 1979 essay collection *The White Album*. She continues: "I have trouble making certain connections. I have trouble maintaining the basic notion that keeping promises matters in a world where everything I was taught seems beside the point. The point itself seems increasingly obscure."

I remember reading those sentences in that early summer of 1980, just days after devouring *Slouching* (I read the two books back to back, which may be why I think of them as companion volumes), and telling myself, *Yes, that's it precisely, that's the story of our time.* The center does not hold, bad things happen to good people, and the consolations of narrative are shaky at best. This would seem to contradict Didion's signature line from *The White Album*: "We tell ourselves stories in order to live." But even that lovely sentiment doesn't tell the entire story, as Didion clarifies in the next, less quotable paragraph: "Or at least we do for a while."

Indeed, this tension between the need for narrative and the narrative-resistant atomization of our culture is the engine that drives *Slouching Towards Bethlehem*. Again and again we sense Didion's subjects clinging to a shred of story, to some idea of the way things *ought* to be done.

When, late in "Some Dreamers of the Golden Dream," Lucille Miller is convicted of killing her husband, her confidante Sandy Slagle starts to scream in the courtroom. "Sandy, for God's sake please *don't*," Lucille pleads, as if there were a decorum for her situation—as if the worst thing imaginable would be to make a scene. "Marrying Absurd" highlights a different sort of disassociation, between the tinseled banality of the Las Vegas marriage mill and the desire, still prevalent in the America of the mid-1960s, to get married in "a candlelight satin Priscilla of Boston wedding dress with Chantilly lace insets, tapered sleeves and a detachable modified train." At first glance, this essay seems to be no more than an anthropological fluff piece. For Didion, though, it's another chance to explore the yawning gap between who we are and who we think we are, between those stories we tell ourselves and the ways we actually live.

Is there a way to resolve this? *Slouching* doesn't offer much in the way of hope. One can always surrender to nostalgia for a kinder, gentler, less fragmented era. Didion herself is not immune to this impulse, even as she recognizes the fleeting nature of its charms. "John Wayne: A Love Song," ostensibly a report from the set of *The Sons of Katie Elder*, becomes an unlikely evocation of her own feelings of loss and longing. "As it happened," she writes, "I did not grow up to be the kind of woman who is the heroine in a Western, and although the men I have known have had many virtues and have taken me to live in many places I have come to love, they have never been John Wayne, and they have never taken me to the bend in the river where the cottonwoods grow. Deep in that part of my heart where the artificial rain forever falls, that is still the line I wait to hear."

The tone in the Wayne piece is reminiscent of "Goodbye to All That," the collection's closing effort, and its most personal: a scabrous account of how the author fell out of love with New York. "It is easy to see the beginnings of things, and harder to see the ends," she insists, then catalogues all the ways her dream (that favorite Didion word) of the city as a kind of cosmopolitan fantasy fell apart. "That was the year, my twenty-eighth," she writes later in the piece, "when I was discovering that not all of the promises would be kept, that some things are in fact irrevocable and that it had counted after all, every evasion and every procrastination, every mistake, every word, all of it."

It's impossible, reading that, not to think about the Haight-Ashbury essay my mother so wanted me to absorb. It is an account from ground zero of the splintering of *everything*, the atomization that Didion finds both fascinating and dreadful. Constructed as a series of fragments that don't so much build as circle around each other, like planets around a dead sun, the piece makes narrative out of the absence of narrative. "He came up from Los Angeles some number of weeks ago, he doesn't remember what number," she writes about "a kid, sixteen, seventeen," who has been shooting speed for three days, "and now he'll take off for New York, if he can find a ride. I show him a sign offering a ride to Chicago. He wonders where Chicago is." Even four decades later, the moment leaves us with a feeling of discomfort, an almost physical sense of just how badly things have gone wrong.

This is the story Didion tells throughout the essay, even as she appears to tell no story at all. There is a handful of principals to whom she periodically returns: Max, who "drops a 250- or 350-microgram tab [of acid] every six or seven days," and his teenage girlfriend, Sharon; Arthur Lisch, one of the leaders of the Diggers, who worries that that the influx of runaways to the district will lead to a full-blown humanitarian crisis; Chet Helms, of the Family Dog, who in one of the essay's most revealing asides informs Didion that "fifty percent of the population is or will be under twenty-five" and "they got twenty billion irresponsible dollars to spend." (Long live the revolution, indeed.) The structure is loose, even rambling. Yet the chance encounters prompt some of Didion's most incisive commentary. At one point, she meets a pair of teenage runaways, Jeff and Debbie, and eventually notes:

> We were seeing the desperate attempt of a handful of pathetically unequipped children to create a community in a social vacuum. Once we had seen these children, we could no longer overlook the vacuum, no longer pretend that the society's atomization could be reversed. At some point between 1945 and 1967, we had somehow neglected to tell these children the rules of the game we happened to be playing. Maybe we had stopped believing in the rules ourselves, maybe we were having a collective failure of nerve about the game. Maybe there were just too few people around to do the telling.

This is the warning my mother meant to give me, although it was unnecessary in the end. As much as I wanted to think of myself as a stepchild of the revolution, I was not wired for a nihilism so profound. In the penultimate scene of "Slouching Towards Bethelehem," Didion meets a five-year-old named Susan who "lives with her mother and some other people, just got over the measles, wants a bicycle for Christmas, and particularly likes Coca-Cola, ice cream, Marty in the Jefferson Airplane, Bob in the Grateful Dead, and the beach." Susan is also tripping on LSD.

"For a year now her mother has given her both acid and peyote," Didion writes, in her usual tone of sun-bleached neutrality. "Susan describes it as getting stoned." Then, for the only time in the essay—*in the collection*—her mask of cool detachment drops. "I start to ask if any of the other children in High Kindergarten get stoned, but I falter at the key words." It's a simple moment. All these years later, however, it evokes the depth of the breakdown, the cost of the fragmentation, the loss of the narrative.

Slouching Towards Bethlehem is undoubtedly a document of its time, but it also has a lot to say about the present, by telling us how we got to where we are. Barack Obama is one descendant of the cultural shift Didion traces in these pages, with his patchwork story, self-constructed and stitched together by sheer intention. Sarah Palin, with her blatant disregard for history, her cynical faith in her constituency's willingness to forget, is another. The birthers and the 9/11 conspiracy theorists exemplify our lack of common narrative, as well as the notion that belief alone is now enough, in certain quarters, to make something true. "How much of it actually happened?" Didion asks at one point. "Did any of it? Why do I keep a notebook at all? It is easy to deceive oneself on all those scores." If *Slouching Towards Bethlehem* has anything to tell us, it's that these questions remain as elusive as when Didion first posed them, in an era much like this one, when, as Yeats would have it, we no longer know "what rough beast, its hour come round at last, / Slouches towards Bethlehem to be born."

163

Justin Peters

PETER FLEMING'S
BRAZILIAN ADVENTURE

In April 1925, a fifty-seven-year-old British explorer named Percy Harrison Fawcett trooped into the Brazilian jungle for the last time. Fawcett had spent much of his adult life under mosquito netting there, and he had become convinced that the region held the remnants of a great lost city—the stronghold of a vanished civilization. Hobbled by age and by poverty, he nonetheless convinced his financial backers to give him one last chance to prove his claims. Equipped with little except a reputation as the man whom the jungle could not kill, Colonel Fawcett and two younger companions set off on a path that would lead them deep inside the remote and rugged region known as Mato Grosso. The party was never heard from again.

Over the next several years, the world press speculated wildly on Fawcett's fate. He had been murdered by hostile Indians; he was being held prisoner; he had lost his mind and gone native; he had been made into a god. Seven years after the explorer's disappearance, a young British journalist set out to find him.

Peter Fleming wasn't the first to go looking for Fawcett, but he was almost certainly the least prepared. A twenty-five-year-old literary editor at the *Spectator*, recently graduated from Oxford, he was a man of the pen, not the machete. He had a taste for adventure, as young men do, but had indulged it sparingly, and had little experience with map-making, Portuguese-speaking, piranha-avoiding, or any other skill that might prove useful in the jungle. His companions—wealthy sons of Eton, men of good breeding and bad judgment—were similarly young and green. "There are, I suppose, expeditions and expeditions," wrote Fleming, and "it looked as if ours was not going to qualify for either category."

Of the expedition, the best that can be said is that nobody died. Fleming and his cohort were slowed at the first when they arrived in the middle of a revolution, and slowed later on by argument and insurrection. Their cartographic ambitions were thwarted when they ditched their surveying equipment, finding it too heavy to carry. They found neither the lost colonel nor his lost city, although they did encounter assorted missionaries, Dutchmen, and "young men of good birth from São Paulo." As Fleming put it: "Beyond the completion of a 3,000-mile journey, mostly under amusing conditions, through a little-known part of the world, and the discovery of one new tributary to a tributary to a tributary of the Amazon, nothing of importance was achieved."

It did, however, produce *Brazilian Adventure*, Fleming's enduring account of the misbegotten journey, which made it all worthwhile. A bestseller upon its initial appearance, the book stayed in print for decades on the strength of Fleming's pungent wit and observational powers.

Almost eighty years later, the book is nearly forgotten, and Fleming's reputation has been eclipsed by that of his brother, Ian, the creator of James Bond. In David Grann's recent *The Lost City of Z*, which introduced the Fawcett story to a new generation, Fleming merits only one direct mention. But in its day, *Brazilian Adventure* was hugely influential. With a journalist's eye and an ironist's heart, Fleming wrote plainly and honestly about his misadventures, his unprecedented candor and self-deprecation reinvigorating a literary genre that too often trafficked in banality, fatuity, and romantic bombast.

"Truth is a perishable commodity; considerable care must be exercised in shipping it across the world," wrote Fleming. The first truly modern travelers' narrative, *Brazilian Adventure* treated the hazards of the jungle as a matter for comedy rather than terror, and suggested that the strangest things about faraway, desperate lands were often the men who rushed over to explore them.

* * *

To call Peter Fleming an unlikely adventurer is to misunderstand the era in which he was raised. Indeed, for that era, he was as likely an adven-

turer as anyone else. Born to wealthy parents in 1907, Fleming grew up
in the sort of bourgeois mercantile comfort that he would spend much of
his life actively escaping. At Eton and Oxford, he won fame writing for
student publications and acting in amateur theatricals. (His biographer,
Duff Hart-Davis, mentions an unconvincing Iago, for which Fleming employed a bizarre staccato cadence straight out of a pulp detective movie.)
In the fall of 1929, his mother commandeered him into a Wall Street posi-

tion. Fleming sailed for New York, arriving just in time for the collapse
of the markets and the rise of the hobo-based economy. Things just got
worse after this inauspicious start, and he returned to England the next
year, cheerfully leaving business behind forever.

After a brief idle spell, Fleming found work at the *Spectator*. At the
time, the long-lived weekly magazine was known for its sterling reputation, but not for its editorial energy. The job turned out to be an awkward
fit. Hart-Davis writes that Fleming "began producing articles of such incisive wit and cynicism that the older hands on the paper became seriously alarmed." His bosses were perhaps relieved when Fleming informed
them that he had been selected as an honorary secretary for a British trade
mission to China, and would require a four-month leave of absence. He
returned to England the next year and resumed his blithe assault on the
Spectator's masthead, inventing a contributor named "Walter B. Tizzard"
and using the name to sign a series of opinionated reviews. But the China
trip made him hunger for more adventurous pastimes.

And so he devoured a notice in the *Times of London* in April 1932,
promising adventure and amusement in the wilds of Brazil. "It is easy to
attract public attention to any exploit which is at once highly improbable and absolutely useless," wrote Fleming. The advertisement, which ran
in the paper's "Agony Column" devoted to missing relatives and friends,
seemed to fall into both categories: "Exploring and sporting expedition,
under experienced guidance, leaving England June, to explore rivers Central Brazil, if possible ascertain fate Colonel Fawcett; abundance game, big
and small; exceptional fishing; room two more guns; highest references
expected and given."

Fleming felt that the ad had "the right improbable ring to it." Today,
its clipped and credulous pomposity reads as an artifact of the golden age
of dilettante exploration. Adventure travel, of course, has always been a
romantic's pursuit. Yet such romantics were unusually thick on the ground

during the late nineteenth and early twentieth centuries. Weaned on the melodramatic novels of H. Rider Haggard, flush with the free time and money granted to those on the right side of the industrial age, these men trekked across the lesser-known continents, hoisting the standards of geography, and ethnology, and science, however loosely defined.

"Nowadays, being an explorer is a trade, which consists not, as one might think, in discovering hitherto unknown facts after years of study, but in covering a great many miles and assembling lantern-slides or motion pictures, preferably in colour, so as to fill a hall with an audience for several days in succession," lamented the anthropologist Claude Lévi-Strauss, who would himself visit Mato Grosso a few years after Fleming. Such explorers did win significant fame, bestowed indiscriminately by a pre-mass-media public eager for exotica. Their travels were lauded—and often financed—by the press, which knew that danger porn sold newspapers. Their findings, most of the time, were of very little practical use.

Even so, these travelers were generally quite serious about their own ambitions, as if their efforts to map some irrelevant river put them in the same class as Pizarro or Cortés. The books that resulted from their South American travels were cut from the same dull cloth. In 1913, having failed to win the presidency as the candidate of the Bull Moose Party, an aged and remarkably ill-prepared Theodore Roosevelt set out on a Brazilian expedition. His book, *Through the Brazilian Wilderness*, explained how he had plumbed the darkest interior, inspired the government to spruce up the Rio da Dúvida with a new name (Rio Roosevelt), and faced down the deadly piranha: "The rabid, furious snaps drive the teeth through flesh and bone. The head with its short muzzle, staring malignant eyes, and gaping, cruelly armed jaws, is the embodiment of evil ferocity; and the actions of the fish exactly match its looks." ("All one can say," writes John Ure in *Trespassers on the Amazon*, "is that his companions did not begrudge him his final fling.")

Roosevelt was preceded by the flamboyant writer and explorer Henry Savage Landor, who, according to David Grann, roamed the Brazilian interior "dressed as if he were heading off to a luncheon in Piccadilly Circus." Landor's own *Across Unknown South America* combines a bluff and imperious tone with the narrative verve of a shipping manifest. When not describing the scenery in slide-show fashion or endlessly marking the changes in elevation, the author complains of the country's inadequate accommodations and the "contemptible imbeciles" with whom he was forced to travel. Landor's men "mutinied and nearly shot him," writes Grann; any of us would have done the same.

Most relevant to Fleming's ambitions was G. M. Dyott, an Englishman who, in 1928, led a widely publicized expedition to find the vanished Colonel Fawcett. *Man Hunting in the Jungle*, his account of the trip, is written from the perspective of someone who very much wants you to know how much he suffered while in transit. Dyott sets the tone with the frontispiece, a ominous photograph of tangled vines captioned, "The Jungle greets you with a Hangman's Noose." He takes enormous pleasure in listing the hazards that he faced, noting early on that "some jungle malady may grip your flabby body from within and snuff out life quicker than the wind disposes of a lighted candle." It is tedious stuff, and the reader occasionally wishes that Dyott's prediction had come true.

* * *

Peter Fleming was not at all this sort of person. But he was greatly amused by those who were. And so he signed onto the expedition as a special correspondent for the *Times*. After securing a book contract and recruiting a companion—a lanky surveyor and Oxford grad named Roger Pettiward, who would later find fame as a cartoonist under the pseudonym Paul Crum—Fleming left his job at the *Spectator* ("the act of a madman," he put it) and headed for Brazil with high spirits and low expectations.

The party sailed in the late spring of 1932, toting shotguns, revolvers, tear-gas bombs, a bull mastiff named Boris, a gramophone, the organizer's father, the organizer's father's chauffeur, and several obsolete maps. At first, finding Fawcett was a secondary goal of the expedition. In fact, most members of Fleming's party were under the impression that they were on a simple hunting trip. But after docking in Rio, Fleming insisted everyone sign a "gentleman's agreement" asserting that their primary objective was to locate the missing colonel, to which his fellows uneasily assented. ("We shared a working knowledge of firearms, and a more or less keen interest in the habits of wild animals and birds: but by no stretch of the imagination could ours be considered a scientific expedition," wrote organizer Robert Churchward in his apologetic account of the journey, *Wilderness of Fools*.)

Fleming and his companions reached São Paulo just as a revolution was breaking out in Brazil—which, characteristically, they did not notice. As the author recounts:

When we got back to our hotel, they told us there had been a revolution. . . . None of us had had any previous experience of revolutions; but from all we had heard of them, to be in the middle of one and not to know anything about it until eighteen hours after it had started seemed to argue a certain want of perspicacity.

The expedition soon met up with its Brazil-based guide, a limping and blustery Australian with a fierce hatred of the press. Major Pingle, as Fleming dubbed him, is an enduring comic creation. Unaware that the expedition members had a real interest in tracking Colonel Fawcett, and unwilling to help them do so when he realized their intentions, Major Pingle led Fleming and his party a short ways into the jungle before announcing that he would go no further, ostensibly for reasons of safety.

Fleming would have none of it. Determined to bring a good story back for the *Times*, he and a few other men broke off from the group and marched toward the area where they had reason to believe that Fawcett was last seen. They found nothing. Then, running out of food and fearing the start of the rainy season, they turned back and rejoined the rest of the party. Pingle, furious at their earlier defection, gave them a mere ten pounds to fund their thousand-mile trip back to Bélem, on the banks of the Amazon estuary.

The rest of the book concerns Fleming's efforts to race Pingle back to civilization, both out of spite and in order to prevent the bilious guide from giving a misleading account of events. They beat him by mere hours, and, after a stop to see the British consul to negotiate a détente, Fleming and company returned to England, none the worse (or wiser) for the wear. An elaborately nonchalant telegram he sent his friend Rupert Hart-Davis before boarding the ship sums it all up: "back twenty-seventh . . . fierce fun abounding health stark melodrama no mail money luggage or regrets."

Even though nothing much happened to Peter Fleming in Brazil, he still enjoyed himself thoroughly. He made lots of undergraduate jokes, picked up some Portuguese, got a little bit better at rowing, climbed some trees. He met some savages, who weren't very savage, and dodged snakes, fish, and insects, which were annoyances rather than nemeses. All in all, the terrors of the jungle were fairly benign, and the genius of *Brazilian Adventure* is that Fleming made no attempt to hide this.

As a result, the book seems entirely real, even in its silliest moments. Fleming himself called *Brazilian Adventure* "probably the most veracious travel book ever written; and it is certainly the least instructive." At no point does the reader sense that Fleming is exaggerating his adventures for dramatic effect, or dwelling too long on the dangers that he faced. (Instead, he occasionally goes too far in the other direction.) "There is little awe left current in the world, and little of that little is well bestowed," he writes. Fleming seems determined to save his awe for those things that really deserve it.

Compared to other South American travelogues of the era, *Brazilian Adventure* is most notable for what Fleming soft-pedaled or omitted. He made no great ado about alligators: "The alligator—at any rate the alligator of Central Brazil—is a fraud.... If he is not a fool and a coward, he might just as well be, so assiduously hidden are his cunning and his courage." Unlike Roosevelt, he paid little heed to piranhas, who "might have been poultry for all the harm we took walking among them." Unlike Landor, he brushed off the region's swarming insects: "It is, of course, damaging to one's self-respect to find oneself dotted with insects against whom popular prejudice is so strong that I begin to wonder whether I should ever have mentioned them at all. But one's self-respect was the only thing that suffered, for they caused no pain or irritation." And unlike almost everyone who had come before him, he concluded that the journey's strains actually made for a fundamentally pleasant experience.

Musing over why his experience of Brazil was different from that of his predecessors, he notes: "If a country contains regions very remote and almost unknown, everyone conspires to paint them in the most lurid colours possible, for two very good reasons: the few men who have been to them naturally want to make a good story out of their experiences, and the many inhabitants of the country who might have been to them like to have a good excuse for not having done so." It takes a tremendously confident writer to do this, to trust that you can make a good story out of your experiences without resorting to embellishment. Fleming saw no reason to elevate natural phenomena to grandiose proportions; it was a failed and embarrassing tactic employed by the Pingles of the world, a style wholly unsuited for the modern age. And even during the trip itself, he made frequent mockery of such manly fustian by conversing in an exaggerated explorer's patois. Water was always "The Precious Fluid." A pistol shot was "the well-known bark of a Mauser." (Churchward's book indicates just how annoying this must have been to the other travelers.) By rendering ridiculous the standard clichés, Fleming allowed himself to slip the constraints of lantern-slide journalism and write about what actually happened.

There are things that are bad about *Brazilian Adventure*. Fleming is an undisciplined narrator, prone to observational excursions that sap the story's momentum. The author's casual racism, though wholly a product of its time, will nonetheless unnerve the modern reader. All in all, it reads very much like what it is: a first book, written in two months and from all appearances not heavily edited.

It is also enormously funny, so that you quickly forgive its flaws. Other British travel narratives of the time (and some earlier ones, such as Captain Marryat's *Diary in America*) are funny too. Yet their humor is principally derived from descriptions of the stupidity of the natives and the inadequacy of the country in which the author traveled. To be sure, Fleming does some of that in *Brazilian Adventure*: he takes much glee in the antics of a drunken and cowardly river pilot whom they engaged to guide them back to Bélem. Still, the book's humor primarily derives from the expedition's haplessness, and the author and his party are almost always the butt of the joke. The pilot may have been drunk and stupid, but without him the Englishmen would have been unable to find their way home.

* * *

The success of *Brazilian Adventure* set Fleming on a career as an international journalist and travel writer. In 1934, he would publish *One's Company*, an account of his travels to China; *News from Tartary*, another book of his Asian travels, followed in 1936. He wrote reams of correspondence for the *Times* and other journals, and he turned to history later in life. But *Brazilian Adventure*, though his first book, remains his best. In it, he took a genre that was often stultifying and pedantic and infused it with grace and comedic understatement.

After Fleming came a flurry of better-written travel books. Evelyn Waugh, who gave *Brazilian Adventure* a positive if qualified review in the *Spectator* ("Mr. Fleming has a really exciting story to tell, but he almost spoils it by going to the extreme limits of deprecation in his anxiety to avoid the pretentious"), would soon publish his humorous account of his travels in Ethiopia. Robert Byron's *The Road to Oxiana* would follow too, as would Graham Greene's *Journey Without Maps* and numerous other first-class works.

The critic Paul Fussell once described the 1920s and 1930s as a time when "a generation of bright young travelers set off from the British Isles to register anew, with all the cockiness of youth, the oddity and exoticism of the world outside." In his day, Fleming was the most prominent and most influential of this pack. By propelling travel writing out of the dregs of romanticism and landing it firmly in the modern era, he offered a new way to approach the wider world. *Brazilian Adventure* should be relished for its drollery and anticlimactic charm. But it is also a document of the time when the era of exploration slid into the era of irony; when the world became smaller and somewhat less new, and bemusement—not amazement—became the standard way to meet it.

Claire Dederer

⟋

BETTY MACDONALD'S
ANYBODY CAN DO ANYTHING

From the time I was nine or ten, I carried a spiral-bound Mead notebook with me at all times. I wanted to be a writer, felt I probably already was a writer, and feared I would never be a writer. I was constantly looking for clues that would tell me that someone like me, someone from Seattle, someone who was a girl, someone who was no one, might be able to write a book. A book that got published.

I was always on the lookout for a message, something that would tell me that this thing could be done. I realize now that what I was looking for was an influence. Influence is a message about what is possible sent by book from one writer to another. Different writers are looking for different messages. As a child, the message I sought was simple: This place is worth writing about.

Just as I was a nobody, Seattle at that time was a nonplace in literature. This was the 1970s. There were few nationally published authors from Seattle. Whenever I encountered any writing at all about the Northwest, I fell upon it gratefully. I was happy to read anything that had blackberries and Puget Sound and Douglas firs and the names of the streets downtown. I read Richard Brautigan stories; Ken Kesey's *Sometimes a Great Notion*, though I didn't even pretend to enjoy it; collections of columns by crabby old *Seattle Post-Intelligencer* newspapermen of the 1950s; poems by

Carolyn Kizer. I read Tom Robbins and was embarrassed by the sex. I read Mary McCarthy's first memoir, but she seemed to hate the place.

And, eventually, I read Betty MacDonald. She had been there all along, on my own shelves, in the form of her familiar, tattered Mrs. Piggle-Wiggle books. Browsing my mother's shelves one summer afternoon, I came upon a grown-up book by MacDonald: *Anybody Can Do Anything*.

I had seen it before but assumed it belonged to the dreary crop of self-help books that had mushroomed on my mother's shelves over the last few years. Bored enough, I picked it up—and found therein an enchanted world. Enchanted because it was exactly real. *Anybody Can Do Anything* is Betty MacDonald's story of how she and her family weathered the Great Depression in an old wood-frame house (not unlike my family's) in the University District (just a mile or two from where I lived). And though my historical circumstances were very different from hers, our shared geography was enough to make me feel that I was seeing my life reflected in her pages.

It's funny to think of a time when Betty MacDonald's books were new to me. Over the years I would come to know them the way I knew houses in my own neighborhood—with a casual intimacy. MacDonald began writing toward the end of her short life, in the 1940s, when she had found happiness with her second husband on their blackberry-ridden acreage on Vashon Island in Puget Sound. Her first book was *The Egg and I*, set in the 1920s. This chronicle of MacDonald's life on an Olympic Peninsula chicken farm with her first husband would become her most famous book, make her a fortune, and form the basis of a wildly successful 1947 film. Next came *Anybody Can Do Anything*, which I held in my hands. This was followed by *The Plague and I*, a surprisingly entertaining account of her stint in a tuberculosis sanitarium just north of Seattle. How she created a ripping yarn out of lying in bed for a year is one of life's mysteries. Finally she wrote *Onions in the Stew*, about life on Vashon Island, which came in 1955, just three years before she succumbed to cancer at the age of forty-nine.

But it was *Anybody Can Do Anything*, with its Seattle locale and its scrappy, cheerful message of survival, which spoke most directly to me. As the depression begins and the book opens, MacDonald has been living on the chicken farm in damp exile from her real life in Seattle. Married at eighteen, she had followed her husband to the Olympic Peninsula so he could live his agrarian dream. Now she has reached her breaking point with the rain, the chickens, the monomaniacal husband, the whole affair. "Finally in March, 1931, after four years of this," she recounts, "I wrote to my family and told them that I hated chickens, I was lonely and I seemed to have married the wrong man." She snatches up her little daughters and makes her long, rainy, difficult way back to the city by foot, bus, and ferry.

There she and her girls are folded happily back into her large family's bosom. Her mother's "eight-room brown-shingled house in the University district was just a modest dwelling in a respectable neighborhood, near good schools and adequate for an ordinary family. To me that night, and always, that shabby house with its broad welcoming porch, dark woodwork, cluttered dining-room plate rail, large fragrant kitchen, easy book-filled firelit living room, four elastic bedrooms . . . represents the ultimate in charm, warmth and luxury."

The book describes life in that teeming, cozy household with her mother, her three sisters, her brother, and her two little girls, plus whoever else might be sleeping over in one of those elastic bedrooms. It also details the literally dozens of weird and none-too-wonderful jobs that Mac-Donald held throughout the depression: hapless secretary to businessmen of every stripe, fur-coat model, photo retoucher, rabbit rancher, firewood stealer, Christmas tree decorator, baby sitter, receptionist to a gangster.

The author jumps from job to job, with whole industries blowing up behind her as she leaves, like Tom Cruise running from an exploding warehouse. She's hustled along in the ever-shrinking job market by her sister Mary, who considers herself an "executive thinker."

Mary has a job ready for Betty as soon as she gets off the bus from the egg farm, never mind that Betty is utterly unqualified. Mary won't hear of such talk. She is quick to admonish her sister: "There are plenty of jobs but the trouble with most people, and I know because I'm always getting jobs for my friends, is that they stay home with the covers pulled up over their heads waiting for some employer to come creeping in looking for them."

The truth of this statement is disproven throughout the book. There were certainly not plenty of jobs. The portrait of depression-era Seattle that emerges is definitively—though quietly—desperate. But on my first read, I hardly clocked the despair. I just thrilled to the evocation of my home, captured in such throwaway phrases as, "There was nothing in sight but wet pavement and wet sky." MacDonald describes places that still existed, that I myself knew—the I. Magnin's at the corner of 6th and Pine, the palatial movie theater named the Neptune. Here she is on the Pike Place Market:

> The Public Market, about three blocks long, crowded and smelling deliciously of baking bread, roasting peanuts, coffee, fresh fish and bananas, blazed with the orange, reds, yellows and greens of fresh succulent fruits and vegetables. From the hundreds of farmer's stalls that lined both sides of the street and extended clear through the block on the east side, Italians, Greeks, Norwegians, Finns, Danes, Japanese and Germans offered their wares. The Italians were the most voluble but the Japanese had the most beautiful vegetables.

Such descriptions caused a strange firing in my brain. I was accustomed to imagining locations from books; there was a deep pleasure in having that necessity for once removed. Even the food they ate was the food we ate. For special treats, MacDonald tells of buying Dungeness crabs and Olympia oysters, just as my family did.

I saw, illustrated perfectly, and in the cold light of nonfiction, the possibility that Seattle might be the setting for a book. I would not be struck so thoroughly by the possibility of a true Northwest literature till I started reading Raymond Carver in the mid-1980s.

My mother told me that Betty MacDonald had died in the 1950s, but that her niece lived in our very own neighborhood. I walked by the house, gazing at it with a true feeling of awe: the niece of an author lived therein! Of course I knew authors were real people. But Betty MacDonald was more than real; she was tangible. She was prima facie evidence that the materials I had at hand—those trees, that rain—were enough.

* * *

Other writers came and went; Betty MacDonald was among those who endured for me. This was because she was funny. No, that's not quite right. Though I didn't have the language for it when I first read her, Betty MacDonald was comic. As I became a writer myself, I studied her, trying to figure out just how she did it.

She wrote long, ridiculous set pieces about her various jobs. She wrote hilarious portraits of her bosses, who in her hands become one long parade of human oddity. She wrote fondly of her family's eccentricities. But above all, she wrote with unflagging self-abasement. Her books twanged with the idea that one's own ridiculousness was comedy enough.

A good example of her rueful tone: "Until I started to night school, my life was one long sweep of mediocrity. While my family and friends were enjoying the distinction of being the prettiest, most popular, best dancer, fastest runner, highest diver, longest breath-holder-under-water, best tennis player, most fearless, owner of the highest arches, tiniest, wittiest, most efficient, one with the most allergies or highest salaried, I had to learn to adjust to remarks such as, 'My, Mary has the most beautiful red hair I've ever seen, it's just like burnished copper and so silky and curly—oh yes, Betty has hair too, hasn't she? I guess it's being so coarse is what makes it look so thick.'" It almost goes without saying that she distinguishes herself in night school by being the absolute worst student in every class.

* * *

MacDonald was master of the comic memoirist's first art: self-deprecation. Other types of memoirists value lyricism, or shock tactics. Comic memoirists are utterly dependent on knowing that they themselves are the silliest people in any given room.

I know whereof I speak—I am this year publishing a memoir about my own very, very ordinary life. Memoirists like me are writing what critic Lorraine Adams has called "nobody" memoirs. As she said in a 2002 piece in the *Washington Times*, such memoirists are "neither generals, statesmen, celebrities, nor their kin."

How, then, to proceed? You're nobody. You want to write a memoir. Your first order of business is to let readers know that you know that they know you're a nobody. So you must imply your unimportance as quickly as possible, and never, ever stop. By means of that simple dynamic, the memoirist makes a friend rather than an enemy of her reader.

In *Anybody Can Do Anything*, MacDonald fails again and again. It's an entire book about failure: her own, and the economy's. It's also about persisting in the face of one's own admitted shortcomings. What she wants is a job commensurate with skills, which she presents as nil: "I wanted some sort of very steady job with a salary, and duties mediocre enough to be congruent with my mediocre ability. I had in mind sort of a combination of janitress, slow typist, and file clerk."

Finally, she washes up safely on the sandbar of government work, taking a job at the Seattle branch of the National Recovery Administration, the New Deal agency started in 1933 and charged with organizing businesses under new fair trade codes. There she felt right at home, surrounded by federal-level incompetence: "There were thousands of us who didn't know what we were doing but we were all doing it in ten copies."

MacDonald is rarely remembered for her wry tone. When she's remembered at all, she is preceded not by her own reputation, but that of the big-screen version of *The Egg and I*, starring Claudette Colbert and Fred MacMurray, which is pretty nearly unwatchable. In the film, Ma and Pa Kettle—neighbors who are fondly, if broadly, drawn in the book—have been turned into tobacco-spitting, raccoon-roasting caricatures. And the public loved them. On the movie poster, the faces of these two crackers loom huge; Colbert and MacMurray cower tinily in the corner. Ma and Pa Kettle proved so popular that eight more films were made about them and their fictional fifteen children, and Betty MacDonald lost all hope of being taken seriously as a writer.

Many years later, I was having dinner with a British writer who had undertaken to write about the Northwest. "You have to be careful about using too much humor, otherwise you end up sounding like Betty MacDonald. Housewife humor," he finished in scathing (if posh) tones. MacDonald has been trapped in this role of domestic lightweight. But her writing, with its quiet irreverence, has more in common with, say, Calvin Trillin or Laurie Colwin than it does with a mid-century housewife humorist like Erma Bombeck. (Though, really, what's so bad about Erma Bombeck?)

What MacDonald models in her writing is actually very freeing—self-deprecation as a kind of passport to the ordinary. With it, you can take your reader into the most mundane details of your life, and they will often go.

I teach adult writing students. When we work on memoir, they want to write pieces about what they've achieved. About their good marriages. About their sterling qualities. "Nobody wants to hear about that except your mother!" I tell them. Which is never very popular. Even so, I try to explain the Betty MacDonald principle to them: what people want to see in the memoir are reflections of their own failures and smallnesses. If you can show readers that you have those same failures, those same smallnesses, and make them laugh about it, they will love you. Or at least like you. Or at least accept you as a fellow nobody.

* * *

These simple things would be enough for me: a story of Seattle; a tale told with self-deprecating humor. But what MacDonald achieves in *Anybody Can Do Anything* is something more than that: a finely observed journalistic record of her time.

The ridiculous set pieces, the fond portraits of her family, and what *New York Times* critic Bosley Crowther called the "earthy tang" of her writing do not seem like indicators of a work of serious journalism. But MacDonald is getting down on paper what she sees happening all across Seattle, and ultimately providing us with a rough draft of history. The details of home and work life accrue, anecdotes pile up, and suddenly the reader has a real sense of daily existence in the West during the 1930s. This is a cheerful, unassuming way of documenting a socially and economically turbulent period. But it's documentation nonetheless.

Take, for example, MacDonald's account of one of her earliest jobs. This chapter encapsulates the uneasiness of the early part of the depression, eerily suggestive of the economic tenterhooks we've been on since 2007. She's been summarily fired from her first job as executive secretary to a miner, so the ever-resourceful Mary has found her a job at her own office, where she works for a lumber magnate. When Betty protests that she hasn't any of the qualifications the lumberman is looking for in a secretary, Mary tells her not to fret. "'You thought you couldn't learn mining,' Mary told me when she installed me as her assistant in the office across the street. 'There's nothing to lumber, it's just a matter of being able to divide everything by twelve.'"

As she makes her way to work each morning, MacDonald is nervous but glad of the work: "Now I grew more and more conscious of the aimlessness and sadness of the people on the street, of the Space for Rent signs, marking the sudden death of businesses, that had sprung up over the city like white crosses on the battlefield and I lifted myself up each morning with timidity and dread."

Her employer's business is clearly failing, but MacDonald feels she shouldn't leave her boss, Mr. Chalmers, in the lurch. She intends to stay until the end. "And I did," we read, "in spite of Mr. Chalmers' telling me many times that the depression was all my fault, the direct result of inferior people like me wearing silk stockings and thinking they were as good as people like him." Again, this blame-the-victim language recalls some of the rhetoric of the 2007 subprime mortgage crisis. But despite the boss's

179

BETTY MACDONALD'S *ANYBODY CAN DO ANYTHING*

efforts to draw a sociological line in the sand, he too is laid low by the economic downturn, and the chapter comes to an abrupt end: "Lumber was over."

The author and her family soon lose their phone service, their electricity, their heat. Being Betty MacDonald, she makes it all sound rather jolly. She tells of endless bowls of vegetable soup eaten by candlelight. And when she complains about being broke, she does it with typical good humor: "There is no getting around the fact that being poor takes getting used to. You have to adjust to the fact that it's no longer a question of what you eat but if you eat."

But sometimes the details tell the story that the tone masks. When the heat and the electricity have been turned off, the family relies upon old Christmas candles for light and firewood for heat: "When we ran out of fireplace wood, Mary unearthed a bucksaw and marched us all down to a city park two blocks away, where we took turns sawing up fallen logs." Here, despite the characteristic pluck, you feel straits getting uncomfortably dire.

This isn't an overlay of social commentary sitting awkwardly atop a narrative. Instead, such commentary is tightly knitted to MacDonald's own experience. When she notices that "every day found a little better class of people selling apples on street corners," she's not making an idle observation—she's wondering if she's next.

When I came to write my own memoir, I was telling a small, personal story about being a mom at the turn of the millennium. I wanted to link the story to larger cultural forces I had observed, to what I saw as a kind of generational obsession with perfect parenting. In Betty MacDonald's writing I once again found just the model I needed. It was possible to connect the larger story around me to my own small story, without pretending to be definitive or historical. In fact, the more I focused on the details of my own very particular experience, the more I could give a feeling of the culture that I swam in.

* * *

The message that Betty MacDonald sent me, through this book, is one of sufficiency: Your small life is enough. Other writers might be looking for a message that will feed their huge ambitions. From books, they learn how far they might go with their own writing. For me, the question has always been: How close to home might I stay?

MacDonald's qualities as a writer—the focus on the very local, the self-deprecating humor, the careful and personal observation of social changes—are modest qualities. They inspire through their very humility. The homely, says Betty MacDonald, is more than enough. This was the message I needed to hear. There's a clue, of course, right there in the title. It's been telling me since I was a girl, right up through the time I became a writer myself: Anybody can do anything. Even this. Even you.

Such lack of pretension doesn't necessarily come with great rewards. There are no monuments to Betty MacDonald. No endowed chairs, no scholarships, not even a public library conference room named after her. But in the shallow green bowl of Chimacum Valley, a two-lane road leads to the chicken farm where MacDonald lived for four tough years. It's been renamed "The Egg and I Road." It veers west from Route 19, cutting through farmland before heading up a hill into some evergreens. It's nothing special. It's just ordinary. It's just a county road.

Contributors

RICK PERLSTEIN is the author of *Nixonland: The Rise of a President and the Fracturing of America* and *Before the Storm: Barry Goldwater and the Unmaking of the American Consensus*.

NICHOLSON BAKER is the author most recently of a novel, *The Anthologist*, as well as *Human Smoke: The Beginnings of World War II, the End of Civilization*.

DALE MAHARIDGE is a journalist and the coauthor of *And Their Children After Them*, which won the Pulitzer Prize for General Non-Fiction in 1990.

ROBERT LIPSYTE'S many books include a memoir, *An Accidental Sportswriter*, and numerous works of fiction for young adults, the most recent being *Center Field*.

MARLA CONE spent eighteen years as an environmental journalist at the *Los Angeles Times*, and is the author of *Silent Snow: The Slow Poisoning of the Arctic*.

BEN YAGODA is the author of *About Town:* The New Yorker *and the World It Made* and *When You Catch an Adjective, Kill It: The Parts of Speech, for Better and/or Worse*.

EVAN CORNOG is a historian whose books include *The Power and the Story: How the Crafted Presidential Narrative Has Determined Political Success from George Washington to George W. Bush*.

TED CONOVER is a distinguished writer-in-residence at New York University's Arthur L. Carter Journalism Institute. His latest book is *The Routes of Man*, about roads.

JACK SHAFER writes and edits the "Press Box" column at Slate.

NARESH FERNANDES is editor in chief of *Time Out India*.

CHRIS LEHMANN is an editor at *Bookforum*, managing editor of Yahoo's News Blog, and the author of *Rich People Things*.

CONNIE SCHULTZ is a columnist for the *Cleveland Plain Dealer*. She won the Pulitzer Prize for Commentary in 2005.

MICHAEL SHAPIRO is a contributing editor to *CJR* and teaches at Columbia's Graduate School of Journalism. His most recent book is *Bottom of the Ninth: Branch Rickey, Casey Stengel, and the Daring Scheme to Save Baseball from Itself.*

DOUGLAS MCCOLLAM is a contributing editor to *CJR*.

SCOTT SHERMAN is a contributing writer at *The Nation* and a contributing editor to *CJR*.

GAL BECKERMAN is a reporter at *The Forward* and the author of *When They Come for Us, We'll Be Gone*, which was awarded the National Jewish Book Award in 2010.

JOHN MAXWELL HAMILTON is the dean of the Manship School of Mass Communication at Louisiana State University and the author of *Journalism's Roving Eye: A History of American Foreign Reporting*.

TOM PIAZZA is a writer living in New Orleans. His books include a novel, *City of Refuge*, and *Why New Orleans Matters*.

THOMAS MALLON is a frequent contributor to *The New Yorker*, *The Atlantic*, and many other magazines, and the author of seven novels and six works of nonfiction.

MILES CORWIN is a former reporter for the *Los Angeles Times*. He teaches literary journalism at the University of California, Irvine, and is the author of a novel, *Kind of Blue*.

DAVID L. ULIN is the book critic for the *Los Angeles Times*, and the author of *The Lost Art of Reading: Why Books Matter in a Distracted Time* and *The Myth of Solid Ground: Earthquakes, Prediction, and the Fault Line Between Reason and Faith*.

JUSTIN PETERS is the managing Web editor of *CJR*.

CLAIRE DEDERER is a regular contributor to *The New York Times* and the author of *Poser: My Life in Twenty-Three Yoga Poses*.